Praise for *Write for Life*

"In this luminous new book, Julia Cameron whisks you so effortlessly along a six-week writing adventure that you will barely notice you have written the first draft of a book until she deposits you back on your doorstep. *Write for Life* is the gust of wind you've been waiting for."

—Mirabai Starr

"A boon to those struggling to get started. Aspiring writers will appreciate the solid advice."

—*Publishers Weekly*

Praise for *Seeking Wisdom*

"Bring your whole self to the journey of this book and you will touch the eternal link between creativity and spirituality. This book will help you come alive."

—Mark Nepo

"I promise you will come away from reading her new book, as I did, with renewed creative zest and energy, as well as insight into your own spiritual possibilities as a creative person. Get this book; it holds magical wisdom and genuine truth."

—Judy Collins

"A must-read for those who struggle finding a connection with a Higher Power, and creatives who want a more robust experience of their art. If you're an artist—and we're all artists—who wants a more dynamic creative experience, you want to purchase and use this book today."

—*New York Journal of Books*

LIVING THE
ARTIST'S WAY

ALSO BY JULIA CAMERON

BOOKS IN THE ARTIST'S WAY SERIES

The Artist's Way

It's Never Too Late to Begin Again

The Artist's Way for Parents (with Emma Lively)

Walking in This World

Finding Water

The Complete Artist's Way

The Artist's Way Workbook

The Artist's Way Every Day

The Artist's Way Morning Pages Journal

The Artist's Date Book (illustrated by Elizabeth Cameron)

Inspirations: Meditations from The Artist's Way

The Listening Path

Seeking Wisdom

Write for Life

OTHER BOOKS ON CREATIVITY

The Prosperous Heart (with Emma Lively)

Prosperity Every Day

The Writing Diet

The Right to Write

The Sound of Paper

The Vein of God

How to Avoid Making Art (or Anything Else You Enjoy) (illustrated by Elizabeth Cameron)

Supplies: A Troubleshooting Guide for Creative Difficulties

The Writer's Life: Insights from The Right to Write

The Artist's Way at Work (with Mark Bryan and Catherine Allen)

Money Drunk, Money Sober (with Mark Bryan)

The Creative Life

PRAYER BOOKS

Answered Prayers

Heart Steps

Blessings

Transitions

Prayers to the Great Creator

BOOKS ON SPIRITUALITY

Safe Journey

Prayers from a Nonbeliever

Letters to a Young Artist

God Is No Laughing Matter

God Is Dog Spelled Backwards (illustrated by Elizabeth Cameron)

Faith and Will

Life Lessons

MEMOIR

Floor Sample: A Creative Memoir

FICTION

Mozart's Ghost

Popcorn: Hollywood Stories
The Dark Room

PLAYS
Public Lives
The Animal in the Trees
Four Roses
Love in the DMZ
Avalon (a musical)
The Medium at Large (a musical)
Magellan (a musical)

POETRY
Prayers for Little Ones
Prayers for the Nature Spirits
The Quiet Animal
This Earth (also an album with Tim
    Wheater)

FEATURE FILM
God's Will (as writer-director)

LIVING THE ARTIST'S WAY

An Intuitive Path to
Greater Creativity

A Six-Week Artist's Way
Program

JULIA CAMERON

ST. MARTIN'S
ESSENTIALS
NEW YORK

First published in the United States by St. Martin's Essentials, an imprint of St. Martin's Publishing Group

www.stmartins.com

The Library of Congress Cataloging- in-Publication Data is available upon request.

ISBN 978-1-250-89758-9 (trade paperback)
ISBN 978-1-250-89759-6 (ebook)

Our books may be purchased in bulk for promotional, educational, or business use. Please contact your local bookseller or the Macmillan Corporate and Premium Sales Department at 1-800-221-7945, extension 5442, or by email at MacmillanSpecialMarkets@macmillan.com.

First Edition: 2024

10 9 8 7 6 5 4 3 2 1

This book is dedicated to Jeannette Aycock,
whose firm belief in guidance bolsters my own

CONTENTS

INTRODUCTION

I'll begin at the beginning. This is a book about guidance, so I'll start with defining "guidance," and answering the most commonly asked questions. What is it? Can anyone receive it? Guidance is direction that comes from a higher source of wisdom than we ordinarily encounter. It is the response of the universe to a question, "What about *X*?" Guidance is available to all of us. It is not the specialty of an elite few. Rather, anyone can ask for guidance and receive it. All that is required is an open mind.

Guidance is the fourth essential Artist's Way tool. *Living the Artist's Way* is a window into my life and my reliance on guidance at every juncture. It's an invitation to use this tool—as I do—to help navigate all areas of your life.

In previous books, I have written about the creative art of listening and prayer, and how we can be led through these practices and through our Morning Pages. Now, I take you one step further. You will see how prayer sets the stage for guidance; how Morning Pages prime us for writing guidance. With *guidance,* we ask on the page and we receive answers on the page. I will show you how this practice has bolstered my life and my art. My guidance and art have become how I think . . . how I make sense of the world. I'm listening for guidance every step of the way.

In this book, I will reveal a personal, vulnerable side, writing about how I use guidance to handle doubts in my life. Ultimately, I experience faith. Indeed, writing guidance makes for a happier, lighter life. It's reassuring; it grounds us and can quell our doubts, anxieties, and fears. It leads to our inner wisdom and authentic selves.

It is my hope in this book to be both charming and calming. I hope you will love the deep exploration and practical application of this essential tool. Maybe my experience will demonstrate that it can be meditative—and *fun*—to write for guidance.

"I wonder about *X*," we may think, and the wondering is a fertile ground for guidance. "What about *X*?" we pose the question, and we find our query being answered. *Something or somebody* responds to us. We "hear" information that satisfies our wondering. Guidance is simple and direct, yet powerful.

Romance, finance, tangled business affairs—all are fair game for guidance. What began for me as a limited affair was soon expanded into an adventure. I found guidance to be far-reaching and trustworthy. The wisdom I had previously sought from human sources was readily available from spiritual sources instead. I well remember my excitement at this discovery. "You mean I could ask about anything?" I exclaimed.

Yes.

And so I did. "What should I write about next?" became a frequent query.

Write about prayer, the answer might come back. Or, *Write about friendships.*

Or, in the case of this book, *Write about guidance. You've been using it for thirty years. Say more.* The guidance was right. I wrote about guidance in *The Artist's Way*, and then spent thirty years writing without mentioning it again, although I was using it at all times. I came to think of it as a fourth essential tool—a sort of safety net that undergirded the three tools I already had in place.

My guidance has pointed me in fruitful directions for more than thirty years. I came to rely upon it. I quickly found that when used in conjunction with the other tools, it yielded me a surefooted path.

And so, a few words about the other tools are appropriate now. When we use all four tools in conjunction, we gain confidence in our creativity. Using the tools we attain a creative life.

THE FOUR ESSENTIAL TOOLS

The four essential tools of a creative recovery include Morning Pages, Artist Dates, Walks, and Writing for Guidance. Used in combination, they have helped people around the world become creatively unblocked, happier, and more productive.

I encourage you to use all four of these tools. This handbook is a deep dive into the fourth essential tool, Writing for Guidance. In diary form, it is a window into how I use it in all aspects of my daily life.

Morning Pages

Three pages of longhand writing, done every morning upon awakening. I recommend 8½ × 11 or A4-sized paper—any smaller, and I find you will crimp your thoughts. As soon as you can after waking up, write three single-sided pages about absolutely anything. If you can't think of anything to write, write "I can't think of anything to write." Yes, you can make coffee first, but don't spend forty-five minutes brewing the perfect cup. The faster you get to the page, the more effective the pages will be.

Very important: these pages are for your eyes only. Show them to no one. They are a completely private place to dream, wish, complain, muse, and dare. They are the bedrock tool of a creative recovery.

Artist Dates

Once a week, take your artist—the youthful, playful part of you that creates—on a solo date. This does not need to be expensive or time consuming. The point is that you commit to a chunk of time where you focus on your artist—and on fun. These mini-adventures are festive excursions that you do alone. It might be a visit to a museum, a solo trip to a new restaurant, a walk through a botanic garden, a movie. An hour or two is enough. Resist your resistance: it is easy to decide you "don't have time" for this date. But artist dates have been known to give us insight, inspiration, and happiness. Choose an outing that enchants your inner artist. Expect your luck to improve and synchronicity to increase as you commit to regular artist dates.

Walks

Twice a week, take yourself for a solo walk, sans music, phone, friends, or dogs. Twenty minutes twice a week is enough to alter your consciousness. You may wish to walk out with a question and see if you return with an answer.

WITH THESE THREE tools in place, we are ready to ask for guidance. Guidance can be sought at any time, day or night, although many people find it best sought directly after Morning Pages. It differs from Morning Pages in that it asks a direct question: "What about X?" Where Morning Pages may yield us information on a troubling issue, they are seldom as direct as guidance, asking point-blank for direction. Here, you have a choice: you can ask for guidance in the same journal you use for Morning Pages, or, perhaps better, in a separate notebook specifically for guidance. A question at a time, we ask, and listen for a response. In guidance, we may ask to understand a thorny issue. A simple sentence may unlock our difficulties. Guidance gives us an overview. A deep dilemma may be revealed and dismissed. For example, I wrote, "What about my writing?" I heard back, *Put sobriety first,* and I realized I was dealing with an issue of faith. My doubt about my writing was actually a failure of trust.

WRITING FOR GUIDANCE

When we write for guidance, we write out a question, and then write down what we "hear." Following our guidance, we find ourselves led, gently and well. As we practice writing for guidance, we find that our guidance comes more and more easily. The novice at guidance may find themselves doubting its validity. "What if it's just my imagination?" It is not, or—if it is—the imagination is far wiser and more benevolent than we had previously thought. The essential message of guidance is the assurance that all is well; difficulties will work out; we are safe, guided, and protected. Our guidance comes, and we come to rely upon it.

INTRODUCTION

The Artist's Way was published in 1992. In that book, I talk about seeking—and relying—on guidance. Laying out a path for others to follow, I talk about the simple practice of asking for—and receiving—guidance. My tone, those many years ago, was matter of fact. Of course it was smart to seek guidance and to trust it.

In the years intervening, I have come to recognize the importance of confidence. We must work to have an open mind. Guidance is trustworthy, but we must do the work to trust. As we seek guidance more and more frequently, we recognize its wisdom on matters large and small. This brings us confidence. We practice having it.

In 1992, I wrote:

Anyone who faithfully writes morning pages will be led to a connection with a source of wisdom within. When I am stuck with a painful situation or problem that I don't think I know how to handle, I will go to the pages and ask for guidance. To do this, I write "LJ" as shorthand for me, "Little Julie," and then I ask my question.

LJ: What should I tell them about this inner wisdom? (Then I listen for the reply and write that down, too.)

ANSWER: You should tell them everyone has a direct dial to God. No one needs to go through an operator. Tell them to try this technique with a problem of their own. They will.

Thirty years later, I still seek guidance. I seek it and—despite my doubts—I trust it. I now have three decades of experience with guidance being trustworthy. And yet I have not written about it as much as the other essential tools. Perhaps I have a lingering fear of being too "woo-woo."

And what exactly do I mean by that? I have a fear of having departed from our accepted rational path. Guidance, after all, lays out a spiritual path, an intuitive path, one taking us to believe in what we cannot, rationally, know. Is it any wonder we feel fearful, lest we be judged a little "touched," a little "crazy"?

Over the years, I've collected my friends carefully. They do not think I'm "crazy," or too woo-woo. Instead, like me, they believe in guidance. Specifically, they believe in my guidance.

"What does your guidance say about that?" my friend Jeannette will ask me when I bring up a tricky issue.

"I don't know. I haven't asked," I will sometimes report miserably.

"Well, I think you'd better check in," she will remind me, trusting my guidance to be accurate. And so I "check in."

My friend Laura Leddy also trusts my guidance. Believing in her own guidance, she also believes in mine. And so, with her, I do not mince words. I say to her, "Guidance tells me," and then I quote what I have been told. Laura listens with interest and no skepticism. I find her belief reinforces my own.

Jacob Nordby, another close friend, is also a believer. He seeks guidance daily and acts on what he hears. To him, my guidance is an accepted fact. When I pursue a direction guidance has given me, he assumes the direction to be correct. We often teach together and our guidance makes each teaching experience easy, even effortless. We live a thousand miles apart but our guidance brings us together across the miles.

Scottie Pierce, a close friend, believes in my guidance and her own. "You're very tuned in," she will assure me. "Your guidance is accurate, sound, and *exact.*" When I ask her to pray for me, she does so gladly, often remarking that I'm "already on the beam."

Nightly, I check in with another friend, Scott Thomas. A Lakota elder and psychotherapist, he invokes his own guidance daily. Writing my daily passage, I often hear from him. "Just happy you're having a creative evening," he'll tell me, trusting that my writing is "led." He keeps his phone calls brief, not wanting to "interrupt the flow."

And so, bolstered in my belief by my friends' belief, I write out guidance nightly. I ask to hear from the Great Creator, and I ask also to hear from Higher Forces. My requests for guidance are always answered and those answers guide my life.

When I teach the tool of written guidance, the most common

question I am asked is "What if it's just my imagination?" To that I reply, "Well then, your imagination is much more helpful and positive than you have thought."

This book is my answer to this common question: "What if it's just my imagination?" This book asks, "What if it's not?"

Thirty years after *The Artist's Way* was published, I am here to report that I still write for guidance daily, and on any topic I need help with. It is a practice I rely on, believe in, and use in every area of my life. *Living the Artist's Way* is a window into my life—and my reliance on guidance at every juncture. As this book lays out how and when I use this tool, it will invite you, too, to apply the technique I depend on to navigate all areas of your life—from your relationships to your environment to your career. It is powerful, it is positive, and it is available to all of us.

Welcome to the creative act of writing for guidance.

WRITING FOR GUIDANCE

I believe in higher realms and higher forces. I believe our world is touched by them, needing only our consent. Swing wide the gate and all manner of spiritual aid rushes to our side. Clang the gate shut again and experience life without headlights. Guidance gives us high beams and we come to rely on them. As we ask to be led, we are led. Write for guidance, and our lives become friendlier. The future no longer looms hostile and un-known. As we ask to be guided we experience a benevolent guiding force, tutoring us as we move forward. This force "speaks" to us in a wise and kindly tone. Difficulties lessen as we are given the grace to handle them. We are *well and carefully led.* There is *no error in our path,* we are assured. We are told, *Do not doubt my goodness,* and our fears lessen. As we take our troubles to the page, our troubles decrease. We write, and a higher hand "rights" things. Calamity gives way to opportunity. Our pen becomes an instrument of good.

"But what about *X*?" we ask, still seeking pessimism. However, optimism meets our hand. There is no trouble that cannot be tempered. Our misgivings, doubt, and despair are met head on. We are promised a sunny future devoid of drama. Our hand, moving across the page, yields us a handmade life. *All is well,* we are told, and we come to believe it. It is a matter of confidence. And confidence is born of practice. We try trusting the small, and we find ourselves trusting the large. "All is well" becomes a mantra. All *is* well, we come to believe.

Guidance comes to us through our own hand. We ask on the page and we receive answers on the page. We grow bold enough to inquire directly and our inquiries are responded to directly. Our guidance is straightforward. "What about *X*?" yields us information about *X*. We are told many things we have no rational way of knowing. Guidance peeks around corners, giving us a glimpse beyond. Our fears and concerns are eased. In the world of guidance, goodness prevails. So many of our fears are groundless, are imaginings. Guidance dismantles these fears, urging us to trust in a benevolent future.

We seek guidance in all arenas of our lives. Romance, finance—no topic is taboo. We ask to hear on a volatile subject and that subject is rendered open to us and without drama. Our wildly vivid imaginings are gently tamed. We will be loved. We will prosper. Guidance assures us our future is bright, not shadowed by fear. Slowly, gradually, we learn we are worthy. Guidance thinks well of us and we strive to do the same. In time, "What about *X*?" becomes drained of drama. Our guidance has offhand optimism and we come to trust it. Writing our guidance out, we reread it for reassurance. We "hear" our guidance over and its kindly tone sinks in.

All will be well, our guidance tells us. We come to trust, at first grudgingly, that this is so. Tutored in equanimity, we find ourselves responding rather than harshly reacting to life's cues. "You're so calm," we are told by our intimates. Our calm is a fruit of guidance. We are rendered more even-tempered. Our perceptions of life have altered. People and events are no longer seen as hostile. We have no need for barbed defenses. The world is not adversarial.

Of course we can pray for guidance and not put our request in writing, but there is something in the act of writing that renders the guidance we receive somehow more "real." It is our hand moving across the page, but our hand is an instrument in the hand of God. As we write for guidance—and write out the guidance we receive—our words may surprise us. They form in our consciousness as though we are taking dictation. A syllable at a time, a word at a time, we are given wisdom. Someone—or something—writes through us. We take down the words we "hear" and are often astonished. There is a wisdom apparent that is not our own. We sense that guidance takes the long view where we—shortsighted—see the short.

"What about *X*?" we query, and our guidance responds not only about *X* but about another issue that has been eddying in our subconscious. I ask for help with my writing, receive it, and hear the additional note, *Your sobriety is solid.* A sober alcoholic for forty-two years now, I had not realized that my sobriety remained for me an issue. Guidance, wiser than my conscious self, kept track of my years of sobriety and my need to remain conscious myself. That my sobriety is "solid" comes to me as welcome news. Guidance tutors me in my priorities.

Do not imagine you are abandoned, guidance chides us. Instead, know that guidance is omnipresent, ever ready to guide and guard us. Opening our minds and hearts to guidance is an act of will. We are willing to be guided, and guided we will be.

"Can I have guidance?" we come to ask, and a flow of guidance comes to us. Listening, writing it out, we may find ourselves surprised by the ease with which it appears. Who told us guidance would be difficult to access? I have found that receiving guidance is surprisingly easy and natural. The more we practice asking for guidance, the more normal it seems. We find ourselves relaxing. We begin to trust the flow of guidance, and further guidance comes to us. *Do not worry that you are off kilter,* we are tutored. *Instead, trust.*

Pen in hand, we transcribe the guidance we are given. Better than merely remembering, we write out our direction. Now we are able to read—and reread—our guidance. The words on the page sink into our psyche. We find ourselves led gently and well.

Over time, seeking guidance at all turns, we come to trust our higher power. Guidance that seems mysterious or abstract proves itself to be, in cozy retrospect, accurate and helpful. And it is a rarity for guidance to seem obscure. Most often it is simple and direct.

"Can I have guidance," we pray, and the prayer is answered promptly. *You are led carefully and well,* we are told, and then the guidance gets more specific. In my case, I am talked to about my writing. *Write about hope. Write about control,* I am tutored, and so when I obey the guidance I am rewarded with writing of strength and clarity.

Write. Write now! I am sometimes urged when I am feeling resistance, not wanting to trust my guidance. Because sometimes I need to be told, *Resist your resistance.* And so I do and when I do I am given work with authenticity and power.

Do not imagine you are abandoned, guidance scolded me yesterday when I was, yes, feeling abandoned. *We are at your side always.* And just who is this mysterious "we"? I have come to think of them simply as "higher forces." I imagine myself talked to by great and benevolent beings. Angels? Who knows. "They" are content to remain anonymous.

Do not doubt our goodness, they remind me, faced with my occasional skepticism. This admonition casts me back through my years of guidance, years in which the guidance proved itself good. I have journal after journal filled with benevolent guidance. *There is no error in your path,* the entries assure me, adding this final comforting thought: *Julia, all is well.*

MY PHONE RINGS. The caller is my fellow writer Jacob Nordby. It has been for him a tumultuous day. His young daughter Meghan has moved out into a place of her own. In her absence, his house feels abruptly empty. Used to being a hands-on parent, Jacob now laments, "I will miss my weird little friend." I sympathize, recalling how it felt when my own daughter, Domenica, flew the nest. That was twenty years ago and the memory still stings.

"I started my book on guidance," I tell Jacob, shifting the conversation to less volatile ground.

"It's certainly timely," Jacob responds. "I think people could really benefit from using guidance right now. Maybe your book will nudge them into trying it," he speculates.

"That would be great," I respond, thinking that Jacob's heartfelt wish may also be guided, giving me just the encouragement I need.

As we ask for guidance, we are well and carefully led. We find our wishes, hopes, and desires being met by the wishes, hopes, and desires of others. Increasingly, we find ourselves to be a worker among workers, a friend among friends. Listening to our guidance, obeying its cues, we have an experience of harmony. Guidance leads us to be an integral part of a larger whole. We experience synchronicity, the delightful intermeshing of our dreams and plans with the plans and dreams of the universe acting benevolently on our behalf. Our "luck" improves and we come to count on it. We are ever more often in the right place at the right time. Chance encounters come to be seen as not chance at all, rather as the deliberate action of the universe on our behalf.

Over time, working with our guidance, we become increasingly cooperative. We are led in positive directions, the precise directions the universe intends. We have a sense of interlocking with the great and glorious gears of destiny. Our guidance gives us cues and we increasingly obey those cues, moving in unexpected directions as we are told. Our hunch or intuition becomes a working part of our mind. We come to depend on it, stepping a step at a time as it directs. "What's next?" we may often query, listening for the subtle lead we are to follow. As we ask to be led, we are led. Seeking guidance, we are guided.

WRITE FOR GUIDANCE

When I teach, I am often met with questions about what to ask for guidance on. The short answer is "anything and everything." A surefire way to discover topics you might benefit from asking for guidance on is to do one of my favorite exercises: the Wish List.

Quickly fill in the following sentences:

1. I wish . . .
2. I wish . . .
3. I wish . . .
4. I wish . . .
5. I wish . . .
6. I wish . . .
7. I wish . . .
8. I wish . . .
9. I wish . . .

10. I wish . . .
11. I wish . . .
12. I wish . . .
13. I wish . . .
14. I wish . . .
15. I wish . . .
16. I wish . . .
17. I wish . . .
18. I wish . . .
19. I wish . . .
20. I most especially wish . . .

Look back at your list. Any of the topics you just listed are fertile ground for guidance.

INVITING GROUNDING

In this first week, I invite you to try writing for guidance. The essays and tasks will help you to look at how you can benefit from using guidance in your immediate surroundings: your most pressing questions, your everyday life, and those people you interact with often. It is my hope that you will discover that there is nothing too small to ask for guidance on—and that your guidance is available, encouraging, and grounding. As you gain strength and faith in your toolkit, you will find yourself feeling steadier as you sense the support of what I call "higher forces."

BELIEVING FRIENDS

My friend Scottie Pierce asks daily that she be guided. As her day unfolds, she is led, moment by moment. Attentive to the cues of the universe, she cooperates, connecting her actions to the guidance she receives. As a result, her days are indeed filled with ease and joy. When I ask her how she is doing, her reply is "excellent." Guidance is the cause.

When I tell her I'm writing a book on guidance, she waxes excited. "Oh, Julia, that's wonderful!" she exclaims. Guidance is a central fact of her life as it is of mine. "Listening to the Divine" sounds to her exactly like what I should be doing. "I heed," Scottie says simply of her obedience to guidance. Heeding, she is graced with a graceful life.

The phone rings and it is my friend Jennifer Bassey calling. She is in sweltering South Florida where the heat and humidity have conspired to prevent her daily walk. "It's simply too hot," she says, missing her regular two-mile jaunt.

When I ask Jennifer to pray for my intentions, she responds by "white-lighting" me—imagining me surrounded in a protective white light, and asking that I be "guided in my words and actions." When Jennifer prays, I do experience guidance. I often

Friendship arises . . . when one man says to another, "What? You too? I thought I was the only one. . . ."

—C. S. LEWIS

There is nothing I would not do for those who are really my friends.

—JANE AUSTEN

ask for her prayers when I teach, that I will be guided as I navigate the needs of the class. Teaching, I am led a word at a time, a tool at a time. When I ask for guidance in the wake of a teaching engagement, I hear back, *Little one, you did well. There is no cause for regret.* And so, bolstered by the optimism of the words, I "let go" and move forward to my next jump.

"I'm always happy to pray for you," Jacob Nordby tells me. And so he prays when I ask and sometimes when I haven't. Jacob relies on his guidance for cues to necessary prayer. He writes guidance every morning and as a result he receives more guidance throughout his day. "You were on my mind this morning," he will tell me. "So I said some extra prayers." Jacob's "extra prayers" are always timely. His guidance for their need is impeccable. When I am worried, I know that Jacob picks up on my concerns. Across the miles from Boise, Idaho, to Santa Fe, New Mexico, he senses agitation and offers prayers for peace. "I believe in higher forces," Jacob tells me. "Call them angels, call them whatever. They act on our behalf." Listening for higher forces, Jacob believes that he receives guidance. "It's a dialogue," he tells me. "I speak to higher forces and higher forces speak back to me."

Jacob would no more forego his guidance than he would skip a meal for bodily health. His guidance is nutritious, he believes, nourishing his spirit. A healthy man, Jacob nurtures himself body, mind, and spirit. His daily written guidance tutors him in self-care. He eats as he is directed to eat. His diet changes as his guidance directs. He recently became vegan, as his guidance directed. Obedient, he reports feeling greater energy and his weight is dropping a few welcome pounds. An excellent cook, he tailors his menus to guidance. The change in diet is "working out well," he reports.

The phone shrills. The caller is my friend Laura Leddy, for twenty-five years an intimate. "You were on my mind," Laura says, her soft voice holding merriment. "I decided to see what you were up to."

"I'm writing about guidance," I tell her.

"Oh, goody," Laura breathes. Guidance is for her a favorite topic. She prays for guidance always and leads her days according to its dictates. "A new book?" she asks.

"How did you know?"

"It's a good topic."

I tell Laura that I have worried about being too "woo-woo." She laughs. Like my friend Jungian analyst Bernice Hill, she believes "woo-woo is where it's at."

"I want to urge people to try guidance," I declare, bold because I'm talking to Laura. "Written guidance is invaluable," I continue. "More people should try it."

"Maybe they will," Laura ventures. "You can be quite persuasive."

"Your mouth to God's ear," I reply.

"Oh, I think people are ready," Laura responds. Her optimism is heartening. Living in conservative Chicago, Laura herself is quietly "woo-woo." She believes in higher forces and turns to them for her many concerns. She prays for family and friends, making a special point to pray for those in need. I often ask her to pray for me and my intentions.

"I'm always glad to pray for you," she tells me. "But I sometimes need a piece of paper to jot down precisely what you've asked."

I picture Laura consulting her jotted notes. Her prayers are precise, careful, as she is herself. A tall, willowy blonde, she exudes grace and good humor. Now I tell her, "So pray for the book."

"Oh, Julia, you know I will," she says, ending our conversation. And I do know she will. Laura has been a stalwart friend for more than two decades.

Now it's my turn to call. I select Jacob, who is reading my recently finished book on prayer.

"So far, so good," he tells me, answering my call and my unasked question. I am eager to hear his opinion. The prayer book was written by listening to guidance. Each day's writing found me picking up a cue and writing what I "heard." The book unfolded smoothly, a guided passage at a time. I wrote the book daily during a cold and snowy winter. Jacob is my first reader and I am on pins and needles awaiting his verdict. An excellent writer himself, I trust him to be discerning. He tells me that he likes the book's opening and that he will read more "soon." "Soon," of course, is not soon enough. Having finished writing the book, I am eager for readers. But not just any readers. Readers whose opinions I value. Hence: Jacob.

"Your book is solid," Jacob tells me now. I'm relieved and delighted.

Outside my living room windows, dusk is settling in. The mountains loom dark and forbidding. Clouds wreath their peaks. It's 7:30 here, 8:30 in Chicago where my daughter Domenica makes her home. It's bedtime for Serafina, her daughter, and I phone to say, "Good night. Sweet dreams." Serafina is restless, not ready for bed, and Domenica has her hands full. Nonetheless, "Mom, I miss you," she carols. "What are you up to?"

"I'm writing my book on guidance," I tell her.

"I absolutely believe in guidance," she volunteers. "Sometimes it's very specific: turn left." Domenica's merry laughter twinkles over the line. "Serafina needs my attention," she says. "We'll have to have a whole conversation about guidance. It's so helpful to write 'I wonder what about *X*.' And then to write on."

"Mommy!" I hear Serafina's plea for attention. Tomorrow is her birthday, the fourth of July. She is wound up, anticipating the day.

"I'll let you go," I tell Domenica, looking forward to her further thoughts on guidance.

A three-quarters moon clears the mountains. Nightfall is upon us. Asking for guidance for a final page of writing, I hear back, *Little one, you've done enough.* Trusting my guidance, I believe I have.

IT'S A HOT and hazy summer's day. The mountains are wreathed in clouds. Rain is pending according to the forecast. It would come as a welcome relief, cooling the sweltering skies. Done in by the heat, my little dog stretches flat out on the cool Saltillo tiles. Out for a brief walk earlier in the day, she came back home panting, eager for her water bowl. My friend Nick Kapustinsky—writer, actor, director, jack of all trades—came by to give me a computer lesson. Too hot to concentrate, I aborted the lesson, talking to Nick instead about guidance.

Nick writes pages every morning. He depends on them to steer his day. His issues and questions are put to the page and in return he receives directives: try this, do that. A skilled poet, he welcomes poetry many mornings, guidance directing him how to shape his verse. His guidance is sometimes picky, tutoring him just what to do in no uncertain terms. A rigorous hiker, he sets out many mornings up the mountains and the mountains become the fodder for his poetry. Lean, muscular, he writes poems to match. He relies upon the daily inspiration that comes to him as he writes pages. Naturally disciplined, he very seldom misses a day's writing.

"I query," he explains and his questions meet with answers. He is open to guidance which is sometimes vague and sometimes quite specific. He acts on its cues and his actions lead to a well-led life.

I would rather walk with a friend in the dark than walk alone in the light.

—HELEN KELLER

Out beyond ideas of
*   wrongdoing and*
*   rightdoing,*
There is a field. I'll meet
*   you there.*
When the soul lies down
*   in that grass,*
The world is too full to
*   talk about.*

—RUMI

"Here, girl. That's a pretty girl," Nick croons to my dog, Lily. She responds ecstatically, leaping up to balance her paws on his leg, "hugging" him. She never shows such ecstasy greeting me.

"It's because she respects you too much," Nick says. Respect or simple reticence, I'm jealous. I want my dog to greet me with such evident glee.

"Fresh water, girl?" I pour Lily an icy bowlful. Nick takes his leave, promising to come back tomorrow at four "for further conversation about guidance."

It's time for me to walk on the treadmill, a fifteen-minute stint, abbreviated from thirty due to the heat. I step on the machine, adjusting the grade and speed to moderate. I have a question I am mulling over and I know that my time on the treadmill will likely yield me an answer. "What place does prayer play?" I am asking. I "hear" my answer.

Prayer sets the stage for guidance, I am told. *But when you ask for guidance, that, in itself, is a prayer.*

It's a matter of receptivity, my guidance on prayer continues. *When you pray, you humble yourself, and humility opens the door to guidance.*

I think of my Morning Pages and the humility they bring, writing freely about anything and everything. Skipping topic to topic, they are, it seems to me, a prolonged prayer for wisdom. We enumerate our concerns and we ponder what to do about them. The pondering is a tacit prayer. "Show me," we are asking the pages.

The request to be shown is a prayer of petition. We are asking the universe for guidance. Without praying formally, we nonetheless are praying. The universe hears our plea for clarity. It responds with hunches, intuitions, direction. We come to understand what our next step is to be. Prayer—for the pages are prayer as well as meditation—has swung open the gate to higher forces. We are led forward. We are led gently and well. So, by humbling ourselves in our pages, we are led to higher wisdom.

WRITE FOR GUIDANCE

Have you tried writing Morning Pages? They are my long-taught creativity tool: three pages of longhand morning writing about anything. They have swung open the door to creativity, inspiration, and, yes, guidance, for the millions of practitioners who use them each day.

I find that Morning Pages prime us for writing for guidance. Tomorrow, upon waking, try writing Morning Pages. See if they don't suggest some topics to ask for guidance on. Choose one, and after doing your MPs, choose something that came up for you, and ask for guidance on it. Write out what you hear.

CAREER GUIDANCE

It's a blue-and-white day but storm clouds gather over the mountains. They sweep downward, bearing their burden of rain. To my delight, heavy drops pelt against my windows. The storm is welcome but brief, cooling off the sweltering skies.

"You look cheerful," Nick Kapustinsky greets me as I swing open the door.

"It's a red-letter day," I reply. I tell him that a long-pending legal matter has just been resolved in my favor. "Cause for joy," I exalt.

Nick doffs his cap and sets to work at the computer. We have congratulatory emails to send out. For the better part of an hour we compose our greetings—notes of thanks to all who helped on my legal matter, a note of thanks to Emma Lively for her canny help on my prayer book. Finally wrapping up with a note to my daughter, Nick and I set out to walk little Lily, grateful that the day's heat has abated thanks to the brief storm.

"I take to the page when I have an issue that's difficult or pressing," Nick resumes yesterday's conversation on guidance.

"I find that writing helps me with clarity," he continues. "The page is a great aid in spelling guidance out."

Posing his dilemmas to the page, Nick finds welcome wisdom. He sums up his practice. "Writing sorts things out."

We have walked Lily up one dirt road and down another. She scampers ahead the length of her leash. Nick and I trudge after in companionable silence. Our walk tuckers me out while Nick, a hiker, seems to gain energy with each footfall.

"I, too, write for clarity," I tell Nick, thinking of the written guidance that told me to write about prayer, a task now completed. If Susan Raihofer continues to love my book it will next go off to my longtime muse and editor, Joel Fotinos. Awaiting his verdict on the prayer book, I will continue to write on the book at hand. The daily mounting up of pages fills me with satisfaction. I am called to write and answering that call brings me peace.

"You know, I can tell when you're writing," Nick breaks into my thoughts. "You exude good will."

I smile to think my writing has a palpable air. On the days when Nick hikes, he, too, exudes good will.

"Well, it's great good news about my book," I tell him now. "My agent is reading and says she loves it. I just hope it holds up well all the way to the end."

"I think it will," Nick says cheerfully.

"I did think the book grew stronger as it went along," I volunteer.

"Well, then. What's to worry about?"

"Nothing, I suppose, but I'll keep worrying until the very end. When my agent says, 'I read your whole book and I loved it.'"

Nick snorts with recognition. Himself a writer, he, too, knows all too well the pins and needles of waiting to hear how a piece of work was received.

"I'll have news for tomorrow," I tell Nick now. To myself I add, "And tonight will be a long night."

Wishing me the best, Nick takes his leave. My phone rings and the caller is my friend and collaborator Emma Lively. I am glad to take her call.

Out of clutter, find simplicity.

—ALBERT EINSTEIN

"Emma," I greet her. "Do you ask for guidance on the page?"

"Ah," Emma says. "Sometimes I do. When I'm worrying about something I go to the page. I listen and write out what I hear."

"Do you ask for guidance on your creative writing projects?" I query further.

"Yes. Sometimes." Emma pauses, waiting for a further question, but I am busy picturing her on her terrace, propped on pillows, taking down what she "heard." I know that Emma writes Morning Pages daily and I am happy to know that she sometimes uses those pages as a source of guidance. Juggling multiple creative projects, a musical and an animated film, she could use the added support of guidance.

"And the rest of the time," I egg Emma on, "do you get guidance?"

"Yes, I do. Something will come to me from out of the blue."

"So written guidance isn't your only form?"

"No, but perhaps it's the best."

I thank Emma for her patience with my questioning. The two-hour difference in our time zones finds me bidding Emma an early good night, so we plan to talk again in the morning. "Sweet dreams," I tell her. "Until tomorrow."

I AM AWAKE early—too early—and the wee hour finds me grumpy. On days when I don't have enough sleep, I am fatigued and I move through my day's jumps groggy and at half steam.

This morning was such a morning, still sleepy despite three mugs of coffee. I dare not drink any more for fear of jitters.

But what's this? An early-morning phone call from my literary agent, Susan Raihofer.

"Julia!" she exclaims. "I love your prayer book!" I had been waiting with bated breath for her verdict. She is a tough, discerning reader. Her approval matters to me. It bodes well for the future of the book. And so, tickled, I burst out: "Goody!"

Getting off the phone, cheered and energized by Susan's enthusiasm, I leaf back through my guidance. The book's next jump is our submission to Joel Fotinos at St. Martin's Press. I read, *Joel will love and appreciate the book.*

I find the guidance optimistic. Of course I am eager to hear tidings straight from Joel's mouth.

Susan phones me back again to say she won't be talking to Joel for several days. "He's a busy man," she comforts me. Writing my Morning Pages, I concur. *It's time to take your foot off the gas,* I write. While I am eager to hear Joel's response, I am ready to defer to his sense of timing. He will get to my book as soon as he is able. And in the meanwhile, I have writing to do.

WRITE FOR GUIDANCE

Choose a topic in your career where you yearn for clarity, support, or direction. Write "What about *X*?" And then listen and write out what you hear. Don't be surprised if the guidance is decidedly succinct, optimistic, and insightful.

Let one not neglect one's own welfare for the sake of another, however great. Clearly understanding one's own welfare, let one be intent upon the good.

—BUDDHA

EMBRACING OPTIMISM

Over the thirty years I have asked for guidance, my guidance has proven itself to be trustworthy. And yet, when the guidance is too optimistic, I catch myself doubting it.

When I teach, I often talk about guidance. I advise my students to try their hand at getting guidance. And they do try it. I tell them my simple formula: three pages of Morning Pages to swing open the door and render myself receptive, then a direct query requesting guidance. I write "LJ"—short for "Little Julie." Then I make my request. Whether I'm addressing the "higher power" or simply "higher forces," I am always greeted warmly. The guidance that comes through is heartwarmingly direct. I am reassured—*You are well and carefully led*—and then the guidance turns to the matter at hand: *Your book goes into loving hands.*

Reading back over my guidance, I find it positive and even nurturing. Its tone is calm and even-handed. Writing by hand, I find myself led word to word. I "hear" my guidance as words and phrases forming in my consciousness. It's more like taking dictation than writing. There is a smooth flow of information only stuttering when I find a statement too good to be true—when my skeptic wakes up.

Make no mistake: believing the positive is a challenge. We each have a ceiling on how much good we are able—or willing—to accept. When something violates that ceiling, being a good greater than our self-worth might allow, we often turn the notion aside. We fear our guidance is leading us in a flight of fancy. We feel foolish as if we are egotistical, "daring" to dream large. If our guidance persists in the positive—as it often does—we may find ourselves resisting guidance entirely. We struggle along, perhaps mired by depression. Finally cornered by our melancholy, we try guidance again and, this time, when the guidance is positive, we grasp ahold of it as the drowning grabs a lifesaver. Our depression lifts and we find ourselves rendered more positive. If we still don't trust the optimism of our guidance, we prefer it to the darkness of discounting what we are told. We learn that we do better to deliberately focus on the positive. Listening, however reluctantly, to our guidance, we conclude in the face of our skepticism that the future may be bright after all.

THE MOON IS rising over the mountains. It is a new moon and its slender crescent casts a sickle from the sky. I am totaling up the day's positives, a practice I learned from my friend Jeannette. High on the list of the daily positives is this one: I walked my dog. Today's heat was oppressive and I planned for only the shortest of walks. Lily, Nick, and I set out in the sweltering heat but soon encountered a welcome breeze. "Shall we try to go farther?" I asked Nick. I had told him our walk would be brief.

"Whatever you like," Nick answered. A rugged man, he was able to withstand the ninety-degree weather. His pace was deliberate.

Hide not your Talents, they for Use were made.

What's a Sun-Dial in the Shade!

—BENJAMIN FRANKLIN

"Let's go for it," I said, and so Nick, Lily, and I trudged onward up a long hill. We would walk a half mile up a dirt road. As we passed a fenced yard, a captive dog set to barking. Lily woofed in response but kept on walking, nose into the breeze.

"How are you doing on your guidance book?" Nick asked me, setting one foot in front of the other, waiting patiently for my answer.

"It's going well," I answered. "I'm on page twenty-five. Do you get guidance when you hike?" I thought the answer would be "yes," but Nick surprised me.

"Not so much," he said. "There's too much exertion. When I simply walk, not hike, I may get some guidance, but most often, guidance comes to me as I write. Yes, writing opens the door."

Blame it on the heat; I found myself devoid of guidance as Nick, Lily, and I pressed on. Stopping to catch my breath, I noted my mind was an empty slate. Nick was right that too much exertion squelched guidance. I turned back toward home, thinking of nothing but the next footfall. We reached my courtyard gate and scrambled down the steps to my garden. My roses were drooping in the heat.

Inside the house, Nick refilled Lily's water bowl, crooning, "Good girl, have another drink." Satisfied that her thirst was slaked, he bid his goodbyes, off to cook a gourmet meal for his family.

"Walked Lily," I note in my journal. The moon is higher in the sky as I write. "Worked out with Michele," I add. And then "Walked on the treadmill despite the heat." All in all, my day was filled with positives. On the whole, the practice made me a more positive person. It reduced my all-or-nothing thinking. Where before I would scold myself for failing, I now praised myself for succeeding. I noticed that every day contained some positives. It began to seem to me that the positives outweighed the negatives. Focusing on what I had accomplished rather than what I had failed to accomplish, I found myself holding depression at bay. Optimism replaced pessimism. Hope for the future—a future built on cumulative positive days—began to replace my feelings of foreboding. Jeannette urged me to focus on the things I could control. Doing this, I found myself feeling less a victim of circumstances and more a master of my fate. "What I can control" might be something small, yet the small somethings added up. At day's end, I had a list of positives. The balance sheet tipped in my favor.

WRITE FOR GUIDANCE

Look back over your guidance. Is it optimistic? Comforting? Helpful?

List three positives from this week. List three positives from today.

Fill in the following:

1. If I could embrace the positive, I would believe . . .
2. If I could embrace the positive, I would hope for . . .
3. If I could embrace the positive, I would try . . .

Count the roses, not the thorns.

—MATSHONA DHLIWAYO

THE HOME ENVIRONMENT

Today was a sweltering day. My normally temperate adobe home was hot and humid. I don't have air conditioning, but I do have a large fan. Moving it from room to room as I myself moved, I was able to offset the heat. I was practicing Jeannette's advice to "focus on the things you can control." Now, as the sun sets, the temperature drops and my home grows comfortable. Talking to my friend Laura, I learned that Chicago, too, was undergoing a heatwave. It was too hot today for her to venture outside. Instead she stayed in, basking under air conditioning.

"Thank God for the cooling," Laura breathed. She made a conscious habit of focusing on the positive.

"Do you write for guidance?" I asked her.

"Oh, I know I should and at times I have, but for right now your question is a good reminder."

"Yes, I think writing helps," I told Laura gently. "I write for guidance daily and it keeps me on an even keel."

"Maybe I'll try it again," Laura volunteered. I heard resolution in her voice.

Getting off the phone, I myself turned to written guidance. Earlier in the day I had taught a large—two-hundred-plus—Zoom class on Morning Pages. "Can you talk more about guidance?" one student asked, and so I explained my practice: three pages of longhand Morning Pages followed by a request for guidance. I explained that I felt the pages rendered me receptive. "Can I have guidance about X?" I would write, and then I would listen, tuning in to what I heard.

"We think getting guidance is difficult," I explained. "Actually, it's easy. Just listen."

"Will Laura write for guidance?" I asked my own guidance.

That's up to Laura, my guidance answered, reluctant to break her anonymity.

"Well, I hope she does," I wrote on. "Can you guide me myself?"

You need air conditioning, my guidance responded. *Take a cue from Laura.*

And so, unable to spy on my friend's behavior, I moved my big fan yet again and thought about how nice the house would be . . . cooler. Using my serenity prayer, I recognized that the temperature—hot—in my house was something I could change. I would simply need to teach more—and watch my pennies. Tutored by guidance, I decided to try.

Optimism is the cure for negative thoughts.

—MWANANDEKE
KINDEMBO

IT'S NINETY-SIX DEGREES outside and my house is simmering. I have tried to arrange for air conditioning to be installed and I have been told I must wait ten more days before the crew can arrive. I'm angry at the delay. Once I contracted to have the cooling installed I was impatient to have it done with. In the meantime,

I have my fan and large bottles of icy water. My friend Jeannette warns me not to overdo it in the heat. And so, I forego taking Lily for her daily walk. She is restless in the heat and I serve her bowls of cold water. Like me, her appetite is off. She doesn't gobble down her dog food with her usual zest. I ate an early breakfast of oatmeal but I skipped lunch. My plan for the evening includes a late meal but I am not hungry. I am planning to eat to forestall the shakes. The excessive heat finds me shaky.

"Are you drinking enough water?" Emma Lively phones me to ask. A great believer in the benefits of adequate hydration, she pesters me to drink more and more again. I have stocked the refrigerator with bottles of water. I seem to me to be drinking them at an alarming rate. I decide to ask my guidance if I am overdoing it. Here is what I "hear."

Little one, your water intake is critical. As you sweat water out, you must take water in. There is no such thing, in this heat wave, as too much water. You do well to drink large amounts. As you are hydrated, you will find yourself less edgy. You will find that good cheer and sanity are the fruits of enough hydration.

Obedient to my guidance, I pad to the kitchen and retrieve yet another bottle from the refrigerator. Sipping it down, I find myself, as promised, growing calmer. I move my fan from my bedroom to my library. I will work at my computer in the relative cool.

But what's this? My computer is swarmed by tiny ants. I'm reluctant to kill them although that's probably the thing to do. Where did they come from and where are they going? I resign myself to their presence, blowing on the keyboard to clear them away. Ants, heat, my house feels inhospitable. I retreat to the living room and call Emma Lively.

"I've sent you fans," she announces. "They're arriving Monday. In the meantime you can keep moving your big fan from room to room according to where you are."

Emma looks out for me. I am grateful for her care. She often anticipates my needs before I am conscious of them myself. I wouldn't have ordered myself fans and now I find myself looking forward to their arrival. While I wait for the air conditioning, the fans will make my home habitable. Thank you, Emma.

The sun is setting and the temperature is cooling. A half-moon rises above the mountains. "Will you be too hot to sleep?" Emma wants to know.

"I have my big fan," I assure her—and myself. When I bought my house, it was winter and I gave no thought to the approaching heat. Now that it is upon me, I think I was shortsighted. Santa Fe is hot in the summer and I am hot in Santa Fe. My guidance tells me that the fans—and water—will be enough. The current heat wave is forecast to last only until Monday when a welcome cold front will move in.

"Only until Monday," I tell myself. That's two long days away. I move my big fan from the library to the living room where I am perched on the loveseat, writing. I find myself writing about the heat although with the moonrise a welcome breeze stirs the piñon tree, bringing relief at day's end.

I begin to see guidance as an aid to the positives. Throughout my day I discover many small "choice points" where I can consciously choose to be positive. Electing to notice and act on these points, I increasingly feel that I happen to my day instead of my day happening to me. I begin to practice the serenity prayer—"God, grant me the serenity to accept the things I cannot change, the courage to change the things I can, and the wisdom to know the difference." With the aid of this simple prayer, I begin to sort out my days. I no longer waste energy trying to change what I need to accept. The wisdom to parse out what can be changed is focusing—as Jeannette urges—on what I can control. Doing what I can, I learn to realize what I can't. In other words, "to let go and let God."

Those who are considered adventurous by nature are optimists too.

—MWANANDEKE
KINDEMBO

*I had to find love &
inner peace to embrace
my story.*

—KIMBERLY ANNE BELL

I write an email to my friend and publisher Andrew Franklin who is seventy miles north of London, working through COVID from his country house. For a year he has published my work on good faith, contract pending once my legal matters were resolved. Now the legalities are cleared up and our emails wax jubilant. My guidance repeatedly assures me that Andrew is for me *a strong ally.* Trusting that guidance, I write to him often. He writes back lively letters, writerly in tone. "How did you manage to become a publisher instead of a writer?" I ask him. Modest, he turns the compliment aside. As COVID decimated England, I had Andrew in my daily prayers. To date he has been safe and sound.

Settled in to write, I admire the moon. Although only a half, it washes the mountains with silvery light. It lights up my courtyard and my garden where my roses droop but my lilies stand upright despite the heat. Nightfall is welcome. The day's sweltering heat abates. With my big fan going and my bottles of water, I prepare myself for a warm but bearable night. My pajamas are cool and I doff my sweaty clothes with relief. I chide myself not to think about tomorrow. The night is cool enough.

A day at a time, sages urge us to live. And so I heed their advice. Seeking guidance, I put pen to page and write out what I "hear."

Little one, you are on track and much goodness flows to you. Focus on the positive and you will see that you are growing more comfortable. The night brings you growing cool. You will sleep well and comfortably, aided by your fan.

I listen to the guidance with relief. Long years of writing for guidance have taught me that its voice is to be heeded. Tonight I welcome its gentle wisdom. I am indeed growing cooler. Tomorrow's savage heat can wait until tomorrow.

WRITE FOR GUIDANCE

Choose an issue in your home environment that you wish to change. Ask for guidance about this issue, and listen. Write down what you hear. Is there an action to take?

WE ALL HAVE DOUBT

So now it is tomorrow and the heat returns. I receive a phone call from my friend Scottie stating that she drove to Albuquerque where the heat was 105. Santa Fe registered ninety-six and so, hearing Scottie's report, I am grateful for our relative cool.

At twilight, a light breeze stirs the piñon tree. The day is cooling. I have moved my big fan from room to room and little Lily has followed it, basking in its breeze. With the weather in the nineties, I haven't taken her for her daily jaunt.

"It will be cooler tomorrow," I promise her, but she paces impatiently, eager to be out despite the heat. Nick has come to give me a needed computer lesson and he takes mercy on Lily, filling her water bowl with fresh, cold water.

"I can't take you for a walk today, but I can give you love," he croons, stooping to rub Lily's belly. "Treats?" he asks and so he inaugurates a familiar game of tossing Lily liver-flavored crackers. She scrambles to gobble them down, energetic despite the heat.

"That's a good girl, Lily," Nick praises her. She adores Nick and eddies at his knees, soaking up his good vibes.

"I'll see you tomorrow at four," Nick bids me farewell. "And you, too, Lily."

With Nick gone, a long evening stretches ahead. I turn to the page for guidance as to how best to spend it.

You will write freely, my guidance says. *You will have words and ideas.* I am frankly dubious. I'm fresh out of words and ideas. I'm ready to throw in the towel, no more writing tonight, when it occurs to me that doubt is a worthy topic. Why, after so many years, do I still doubt? Guidance chimes in.

It's human nature to doubt, I hear. *A lack of trust is part of the human condition.*

"But why?" I complain.

Your guidance is reliable but your temperament is not. You experience ups and downs.

"But after all this time surely I should trust!" I am now whining.

Trust is elusive.

"But why?"

As a human being you are prone to doubt. It's in your spiritual DNA.

I realize that my guidance is telling me doubt is natural. I resent this but I also realize that it is true. One more time, my guidance is proving itself reliable. It expects me to doubt and it accepts doubt as normal and natural. Faced with this realism, I surrender. All right. I will doubt.

And so I find myself doubting that guidance will give me words and ideas. The only idea that comes to me is a stubborn one: doubt is a character defect. Feeling doubt, I feel shame. A dark cloud colors my temperament. I try to pull myself up by my bootstraps: I won't doubt.

But trying not to doubt leads me to more doubt. Self-scrutiny leads to self-obsession. Self-obsession is painful. Finally,

I journey through life daily, embracing love from where I can and giving love to whom I can.

—KIMBERLY ANNE BELL

The ache for home lives in all of us, the safe place where we can go as we are and not be questioned.

—MAYA ANGELOU

one more time, I surrender. All right. Doubt is normal and natural. Guidance expects it. I am no exception to the human condition.

This brings me to humility. I am being humbled. I am being asked to be a worker among workers, a friend among friends. I am no better than my peers. But I am also no worse. If it is human to doubt guidance, well then, I am human. But what is this? Guidance promised me words and ideas and, lo, I am finding them. In writing about doubt, I am experiencing faith.

You experience ups and downs, guidance told me, and my evening's experience is exactly that.

"Guidance is *accurate,*" I catch myself thinking, doubt temporarily vanquished. But this time I know that it will return again for, as guidance itself said, *A lack of trust is part of the human condition.*

WRITE FOR GUIDANCE

Choose an issue where you are currently experiencing doubt. Take pen to page and ask for guidance on this issue. Do you sense a hint of faith?

QUELLING ANXIETY

It's twilight and a light breeze stirs the piñon tree. The day—an infernally hot day—is cooling. My big fan renders the room bearable. I sip on a bottle of icy water, staring out my windows at the mountains. Clouds crown their peaks. The setting sun tints them apricot. The moon, nearly full, dominates the sky. I have set aside two hours to write and I settle myself on the loveseat, pen in hand, journal ready. I'm writing longhand as is my habit. I find that writing by hand eggs on a flow of words. And so I set pen to page, eager to start. I find myself writing about the mountains' clouds. Do they hold rain? A peal of thunder sounds. Rain would be welcome to contest the heat. My friend Scott telephones. "Did you hear the thunder?" he asks. "We may get rain."

Home is the nicest word there is.

—JOHN HAWKINS AND
WILLIAM PUTMAN

The piñon tree lashes now in a stiff wind. Tiny birds take refuge in its inner branches. Another peal of thunder sounds to the west. "Our weather often comes to us from the west," Scott tells me. "I'm looking for rain, sitting out in my courtyard, staring out over the wall."

Sensing an impending storm, little Lily hides in a corner behind my coatrack. Thunder frightens her. And the thunder is

Landscapes of great wonder and beauty lie under our feet and all around us.

—WALT DISNEY

moving closer. A few heavy drops of rain pelt now against my windows. "Oh, good," I breathe. The heat has been oppressive. I welcome rain.

The phone shrills. The caller is Jennifer Bassey, just tagging base from South Florida. "I'm calling you now because we're going out on our deck for two or three hours and I'm not taking my phone with," she reports. "I just wanted you to know I love you."

Jennifer's call is brief but welcome. I had planned to call her later but now I will wait until tomorrow. I frequently call Jennifer to ask for prayers. "I'm white-lighting you," she prays, and her prayers are potent. When I teach, she prays for my effectiveness. I teach well and call afterward to thank her. "Anytime," she responds.

I picture her on her deck in Florida, enjoying a cigar with her husband, George. They are a well-matched couple, both still youthful and attractive in their seventies. Like Jennifer, George is a powerful pray-er. He prays daily for an hour, never missing a day. Their hours relaxing on their deck are hours of appreciation. Their view is of the intercoastal waterway and the ocean beyond. Great walkers, they hike daily, two to four miles, before coming home to enjoy their deck. They bask in each other's company, a happy twosome, determined optimists, thoughtful friends.

"I'll talk to you tomorrow," Jennifer says, signing off. I look forward to tomorrow's call and a longer check-in. Jennifer's spiritual practice is rigorous yet lighthearted. Her guidance nudges her to be thoughtful of her far-flung friends—thoughtful as she was to me tonight.

The brief rain is over. Lily creeps out from her hiding place and stretches out in the living room on the cool Saltillo tiles. Her flanks pump rhythmically. She is enjoying the cool tiles.

"Is Lily still too hot?" I ask guidance.

Pour her fresh water, I am told.

And so I pad to the kitchen, take an icy bottle of water from the refrigerator, and tip its cold contents into her bowl. In the heat, she has been drinking frequently and deeply, draining her large water bowl in a single sitting. I refresh her bowl.

My plan for the evening's writing was to write about anxiety, but the weather capsized my plan. I meant to say that anxiety could shut down guidance, choking the channel closed through which guidance flowed.

"What should I say about anxiety?" I now ask.

Say that it's deadly, I am told.

Deadly? Isn't that a bit dramatic?

Life without guidance is deadly, my guidance persists, dramatic still.

When you are anxious, you cannot hear, guidance continues, and I find myself coming into agreement, recalling the times I have prayed for guidance and been greeted by static. It is true, I realize, that anxiety is a killer. I think of Jennifer's question to me as we prayed. "Are you anxious? Draw a deep breath and count to five. Do it again. Is your diaphragm relaxing? Now we can pray."

And so, tutored by Jennifer, I learned to release anxiety. "Just breathe," she told me. Breathing deeply now, I hear my guidance. *Anxiety is the enemy. Breathe deep.*

The mountains are misted over. A light rain is falling. The piñon tree glistens with raindrops. The house is cooler thanks to two new fans that Emma sent me. They make a dull roar but I am able to tune it out.

I wrote for guidance earlier in the day and it was greatly reassuring. I asked to hear from the higher power and I heard, *Julia, I am at your side. You are led carefully and correctly.* The guidance was precise and soothing. *There is no cause for anxiety. For tonight I give you words and thoughts.*

And so, settled on my loveseat, I wait for "words and

I believe in intuitions and inspirations. I sometimes feel that I am right. I do not know that I am.

—ALBERT EINSTEIN

Don't try to comprehend with your mind. Your minds are very limited. Use your intuition.

—MADELEINE L'ENGLE

thoughts." I have talked with Scottie, who pronounced herself "excellent." At her house as at mine, a light rain is falling. "The little dogs and I are enjoying the smell of rain," she tells me. I tell her that I have not yet written and she assures me, "It's early yet. There's plenty of time left to write." When we hang up the phone, I think of Scottie's daily prayer for "ease and joy." Clearly, one more day, her prayer has been answered. Her throaty voice is calm as she enquires about *my* day.

"I had a sore back today," I tell her reluctantly. "But it's better now," I quickly add. In the face of Scottie's perpetual good cheer, it is hard to share a negative.

But my back did hurt and still hurts now, but less. I worked out today with my trainer, Michele Warsa, and she put me through a series of stretches aimed at limbering up sore muscles. "You can always perform the stretches on your own," Michele advises me. True enough, but they feel better done with her.

So now my back is aching less and I turn to guidance for further advice. *Do your stretches again,* I am told. *That will bring you relief.*

Grumpy but obedient, I do my stretches. Sure enough, my back feels almost normal. "What would I do without guidance," I catch myself mulling. I have found guidance helpful in all are-nas of my life—reaching back to teaching protocol. When I ask for guidance from higher forces, I am assured, *Don't worry. We will not abandon you. We are ever ready to guide you. Ask us for help and we gladly give it to you.*

And so, reassured, I turn to my day's writing. "Body, mind, and spirit go together," I find myself writing, and I think back over my day's experience that proved that this is so. My sore back caused my mind to worry and my spirit to sag. Looking out the window at my piñon tree, I am briefly cheered by the tiny birds it gives shelter. As always, nature is a balm.

"I walked my puppy a long walk," my daughter, Domenica,

phones to tell me. Her puppy, a Bernedoodle—part Bernese mountain dog, part poodle—is growing huge. Soon she may be walking my daughter, not vice versa. But the day's walk puts my daughter in high spirits.

"I missed my Morning Pages," she confesses. "It's good I got the walk."

My daughter ordinarily does pages daily, relying on them for guidance about her busy days. In addition to pages, she enjoys a wide network of friends who advise her on her daily dilemmas. Today she phoned a girlfriend of two-plus decades for advice on how best to deal with a difficult relative.

"Steer clear of her," the friend advised. "Don't encounter her." And so my daughter is practicing "restraint of tongue and pen." When she tells me the crass hijinks of her spoiled and selfish auntie, I echo her friend's advice to "steer clear." My daughter tells me her written guidance also advises distance. I think to myself how fortunate my daughter is, enjoying guidance in many forms, written and spoken. Catching myself becoming embroiled in my daughter's plight, I myself turn to written guidance and I hear *steer clear*. And so, tutored to keep my distance, I find my anxiety dropping.

I have been writing for guidance for thirty years. In those years my daughter has gone from perky teenager to married matron. How often, in the course of her trajectory, have I taken to the page for parenting advice? Now my daughter is a parent herself and a twenty-year veteran of Morning Pages. Throughout her journey she has availed herself of guidance, writing out "inventory" of her successes and her shortcomings, asking, daily, for wisdom to accept the things she cannot change and the courage to change the things she can. I have watched her working out her life's path. Now happily married to a worthy man, she mothers a boisterous child, Serafina, now eleven, born—and showing it—on Independence Day.

When you reach the end of what you should know, you will be at the beginning of what you should sense.

—KAHLIL GIBRAN

Man is not worried by real problems so much as by his imagined anxieties about real problems.

—EPICTETUS

"So I'm going to steer clear," my daughter concludes our phone call. "Although I was really tempted to tell my aunt off."

"But you won't get involved?"

"No. I won't."

And so, I hang up the phone thinking gratefully of the wisdom guidance provides.

WRITE FOR GUIDANCE

Fill in the following sentences:

1. I am anxious about . . .

2. I worry that . . .

3. My number-one source of anxiety is . . .

Now, choose the most "potent" topic on your list. Write for guidance: What should I do about X? Do new solutions come to mind?

INVITING STRENGTH

This week, you will tap into your guidance on matters of self-care. You will actively seek out the positive in your life and the behaviors—and friends—that will encourage it. You will find that your guidance can lead you to self-care, and that as you commit to self-care, you are given clarity and strength. *Treating yourself like a precious object will make you strong.* As you deepen your commitment to loving self-care, you will find a sense of new self-worth reinforcing your self-loving decisions. You will find yourself setting new boundaries.

LOOKING TO THE POSITIVE

My house has mice. Anthony, my handyman, has set traps. Tonight, he came to check on his traps and discovered two dead mice, one in my living room, one in my bathroom. The mice were dead but they filled me with fear. Were there more? I didn't want to know. I turned to guidance for reassurance.

"What about the mice?" I asked.

You are eradicating the mice, I was told. *Anthony is a huge help and he is thorough. You will be safe. The mice are not a threat.*

And so, though jittery, I settle in to write. I am appreciative, as always, of my guidance. "Eradicating" sounds good to me. I believe that guidance chooses its words with care.

Now I am settled in on the loveseat, looking out the window at the piñon tree which dances lightly in an evening breeze. Visible beyond the tree is a stretch of lawn and beyond the lawn, a vista of the mountains. It's twilight and the mountains are lit with gold. The setting sun gilds their peaks.

My day has been a good one. Susan Raihofer, my literary agent, phoned me with the great good news that my editor, Joel Fotinos, "loved" my new book. I received the news with glee. Guidance had told me that the book would be met with "open arms" but, as I do so often with great good news, I found myself filled with doubt. "I loved it," Joel's email to Susan stated flatly. Susan forwarded the email to me and I read it over several times, willing myself to absorb the glad tidings. "Loved it" was strong language. I had spent the week past on pins and needles awaiting Joel's verdict. Now it was in.

I called my colleague Emma Lively. She had served as editor on the book. "Joel loved it," I bubbled over.

"Congratulations." Emma received the news with enthusiasm. She, too, had spent the week of Joel's deliberations on pins and needles.

My FRIEND SCOTT Thomas, a Lakota elder, begins his day with a request for guidance. Laying out an offering of food and coffee, he asks his Lakota ancestors to steer his day. If he has questions, he asks that they be answered. If he has ongoing issues, he asks that they be resolved. Sober for thirty-four years, he follows a spiritual path that puts him in close contact with the "unseen world," as he calls the realm where spirits dwell. Daily, before the business of the day gets underway, he seeks conscious contact with those who have gone before him.

"The spirits look out for me," Scott explains his ongoing sense of protection. A large man with a calm and gentle manner, Scott wears his long silver hair in a neat plait down his back. Around his neck, he wears a rawhide pouch filled with protective amulets.

"I don't think the English language has words for it," he says. "Once, we had a lot of spiritual terms, but no longer. It's hard to talk about spirits and the unseen world without sounding cuckoo. The invisible world is like a mirror of us—spirit and consciousness. Of course there are spirits who love us and guide us. The idea that when someone dies, all their love for you is gone—poof!—is ridiculous. It makes people afraid of death. It's a terrible belief. I believe that the spirit's love lives on. I know it does. It's easier to explain all of this in Lakota."

Scott talks softly and persuasively of his spiritual beliefs and practices. Praying first thing in the morning, he sets the tone for his day. Throughout the day, his guidance continues, coming to him as a spiritual nudge, a hunch or intuition.

"I'm guided," he says simply. Following his guidance is natural and normal to him. As he says, "Of course there are spirits who love and guide us."

Setting out his morning offerings, Scott signals to the unseen world his belief in it and the spirits who dwell there, ever watchful and protective, ever kind and wise. A therapist by trade, a healer by temperament, Scott blends his native Lakota beliefs with modern therapeutic techniques. Combining Lakota healing ceremonies with psychology, he offers his patients a unique path to mental and spiritual health. Grounded in both Lakota traditions and what he calls "the dominant culture," he enjoys a thriving practice earmarked by deep compassion. Viewing much of modern Western life as barbarous, he tempers his work with an ancient, spiritual lineage. Guidance tutors him in his personal, idiosyncratic way of healing. He is grateful to the spirits that this is so.

Intuition is like reading a word without having to spell it out.

—AGATHA CHRISTIE

A SOUL THAT is early to rise, Emma Lively greets the day on the page. She writes Morning Pages seeking guidance for the day ahead and guidance comes to her through her own hand. "I wonder what to do about *X*," she may mull and, sure enough, the answer will come to her. It may be a definite direction or something more subtle, a hunch or intuition. Over the years

*Totally calm within
himself,
A bhikkhu would not
seek peace from another;
For one who is at peace
with themselves,
There is nothing to hold
on to, still less to put
down.*

—BUDDHA

of her daily practice, Emma has come to trust her guidance. Following it, her life unfolds smoothly, filled with creativity and friends.

"Emma is so sunny," a colleague remarks. "She is such an optimist." It is thanks to her morning practice that Emma is filled with good cheer. She trusts her guidance to lead her well and carefully. When she encounters a difficulty she "takes it to the page." There she receives her answers. Both a writer and a composer, she takes down what she "hears." Her talents are honed through her pages. Guidance gives her inspiration. She flourishes a page at a time.

Victoria, the mother of a small child, is another practitioner of Morning Pages. She rises early, before her child, and takes to the page.

"My days go better when I write," Victoria declares. Her pages are precious to her and on the days when her child wakes first, she misses them.

"Yes, they give me guidance," Victoria testifies. "I write about anything and everything and the pages tell me what to do about my issues." She adds, "I'm training my daughter: Mommy is writing."

Victoria's daughter is catching on. She is learning that on the days when Mommy writes, she is less crabby.

"I sometimes get up at 5:30, just to get my pages done," Victoria confides. Juggling motherhood and a full-time career as a director, Victoria needs all the helpful guidance she can get. Her practice of pages gives her support. "I get my priorities in order," she claims. "I'm told what to do and how to do it."

In addition to her daily practice of pages, Victoria makes a daily habit of what she calls "sanity walks." Setting out from her house, she walks a mile to a neighboring park. Stretching her legs, she unkinks her mind. Mulling over the morning's guidance, she makes an action plan. Returning home aerobicized and energized, she tackles her to-do list. Guidance directs her on what to do first. Raising both her daughter and a newly adopted puppy, her days are filled with many small "jumps." Whether supervising her daughter's piano lesson or teaching the puppy "stay," she finds herself heeding guidance on just how to accomplish the task at hand. Her Morning Pages address the many issues she faces in a day. At day's end, she counts back over her many positives. Guidance has led her to be active and productive. Nightfall finds her tired, but satisfied.

FOR FIFTY-EIGHT YEARS a practitioner of a spiritual path, my friend Julianna McCarthy practices acute listening as a form of guidance. Trained by her practice to help and serve others, she does so by listening, offering a sensitive ear to the trials and tribulations of those she counsels. Blessed with great good humor, she often offers a pithy remark to sum up and dismantle difficulties. Living deliberately "a day at a time," she champions the wisdom to be found in living only each day's march. "How important is it?" she may gently query when faced with an overly dramatic recital of difficulties blown out of proportion. "First things first," she may advise when a caller's life is chaotic due to misplaced priorities. Never overtly religious, she may yet ask pointedly, "Where's God in all this?" Duly chastened, the caller may seek out a spiritual dimension in a seemingly secular problem.

Belief consists in accepting the affirmations of the soul; unbelief, in denying them.

—RALPH WALDO EMERSON

"I cherish Julianna's humor," declares one grateful recipient of her wisdom. "It draws things to scale."

At ninety years of age, Julianna is indeed a sage elder, leading her life with sagacity and grace.

WRITE FOR GUIDANCE

The practice of consciously expressing gratitude is a powerful spiritual tool, and one that also puts us in touch with the power of our guidance. Fill in the following:

1. A person I am grateful for is . . .
2. In my career, I am grateful that . . .
3. I am grateful that my guidance . . .

THE POWER OF SLOWING DOWN

Michael is a high-strung man, at the height of his creative powers in his mid-seventies. Although it is "top secret," he has a pacemaker that steadies his heart. The pacemaker is a help, a "godsend," but it is his practice of meditation that serves him the most.

"I meditate twice a day for twenty minutes," Michael explains. "Before I meditated I was a classic type A personality, always on overdrive. By nature I was a worrier, always fretting over some dire imagining, a scenario of impending doom. When I discovered meditation, I found myself struck calm."

Michael laughs at his own story. He is clearly relieved to be calm. "Before I meditated, I was always racing, dashing from project to project, chasing my own tail. Meditation taught me to slow down. I began to believe there was time. I found I could go a step at a time. The right project would be there when I got there."

Married five times, Michael jumped from spouse to spouse, relationship to relationship. Meditating, he realized he was trading trouble for trouble. "I stopped running," he says now.

"Slowing down, I appreciated my wife. She'd put up with so much from me."

A gifted entrepreneur, Michael always ran through assistants. It took a lot—too much—to keep up with him. He hired and fired at the drop of a hat. "I was impossible," he says bluntly. "I never saw my part in things. I never saw that I drove them to it."

Self-knowledge was, for Michael, a fruit of meditation. He began to see his part in his chaotic life. He began to hear guidance: "The still small voice," he characterizes what he heard.

"I stopped being such a son of a bitch," he says now. "I began to hear softer, gentler ways to do things." To his surprise, his "softer, gentler" ways seemed to work.

For decades a high-profile star in his field, he now became something more than a mere star. He began a practice of mentoring gifted newcomers. Always a character, he now became a man of character. As his manner softened, his always sharp business sense became sharper still. His guidance was cueing him to opportunity.

"I think I'm smarter," Michael claims. "Or perhaps I'm wiser." Smarter or wiser, Michael owes a change of heart to his guidance. Twenty minutes twice a day has given him a fuller, richer life.

"When I slowed down, my luck speeded up," Michael asserts. "Meditation works. Now I count on it."

It's SEVEN THIRTY. The mountains are settling into dark folds. My piñon tree bobs gently in a twilight breeze. It's the end of a long and crabby day. I woke early and was unable to fall back asleep. I got up, tired, and drank two large mugs of coffee hoping to wake up. The coffee was strong but my fatigue was stronger. At noon, I took myself back to bed, hoping for a restorative nap. No such luck. I tossed and turned, sweltering in the midday heat. After a restless hour, I roused myself and tried more coffee. It was as if the caffeine was missing. The coffee had no effect. I faced the remainder of my afternoon tired and cross.

Belatedly, it occurred to me to seek guidance. I was told: *Do not push yourself. This is a day when exertion is counterproductive. Give yourself a break and stop pushing. Your harsh mood will subside if you are gentle with yourself. Drink water. Sit by a fan. Allow yourself to be hydrated and cool. The hot weather has added to your negative mood. So now, rest, relax, and lower the bar.*

My guidance was soothing. I realized that I been pushing myself, striving to be productive despite my mood. Faced with gentle guidance, I let myself off the hook. My friend Scott Thomas phoned me and when he listened to my recital of my irritable woes, he was compassionate. "Julia, some days I am in the flow and other days—like yours today—I am out of synch. Today, after all, is Friday, the end of a long and stressful week. You were waiting to hear the news of your book. Waiting is hard. Your news was good but anticlimactic. Let the week be over and done with."

I was grateful to Scott for his advice. A gifted therapist, he was trained to dismantle anxiety. His words to me were a soothing balm. I found myself thinking how lucky his clients were to experience such gentle compassion. His advice to me: "Slow down."

There is a shift in the weather. While I was on the phone with Scott, an evening rainstorm blew in. My windows were streaked with wet. Little Lily, restless with the storm, paced my living room, seeking refuge. Thunder makes her nervous and this evening's storm featured both thunder and lightning. The rain clouds blotted out the mountains. My piñon tree waved in the wind. Its outer branches lashed to and fro. Its inner branches held steady, offering safe haven to tiny birds. Lily paused in her pacing to stare out the window. A few intrepid ravens flew

You'll never find rainbows if you're looking down.

—CHARLIE CHAPLIN

in circles despite the storm. *Whoosh!* The piñon tree shook its branches. Raindrops glistened in the waning light.

"What should I do with the evening?" I asked guidance, relieved that my sour mood was lifting.

Let yourself write, guidance replied, and so I set my pen to page, recording the weather. The storm was brief. Lily was relaxing, curling at my feet. A few sheets of lightning marked the storm's retreat. The shower had cooled the sweltering heat. In my garden, my proud lilies gratefully drank the drops. My roses drank, too, and the courtyard tiles glistened dark and wet.

"Bravo!" I breathe, happy now in the evening's cool. My mood has shifted from sour to sweet. I let myself simply hang out on the page, staring out my large window at the darkening sky. Lily stirs herself and pads to her dog door. I can sense her debate: "Shall I go out?" She does go out. The storm has left behind a cool mist. After the day's heat, it is welcome. Lily ventures out, then comes back in. Her snowy coat is damp. I pad to the kitchen to check her supplies. She has a bowl of crunchy dog food and an accompanying bowl of water. Satisfied that Lily is well cared for, I close the dog door, locking her in for the night. We are, the two of us, safe and snug. Our mood is happy.

WRITE FOR GUIDANCE

Often, when we slow down, we find that we open the door to guidance and inspiration. It is a paradox that by easing up on ourselves, answers seem to come to us as if out of nowhere, and often with powerful speed.

Ask your guidance what you could do to ease the pressure on yourself. Can you take a break or a nap? Can you push a deadline? Can you give yourself a full day of "no expectations," where you ask for nothing from yourself?

What do you hear? Can you give it a try?

THE INSPIRATION OF FRIENDS

Victoria is in her mid-forties. She has followed a spiritual path since she was twenty-one. Her path teaches meditation as a prime component of spirituality. Meditating daily, Victoria receives guidance. She is obedient to the guidance which comes to her—sometimes as a spoken word, sometimes, more subtly, as a hunch or intuition.

"I believe in guidance," Victoria states. "When I meditate, I open myself to spiritual dimensions. I'm told how to lead my day, leading me a step at a time."

Victoria is the mother of a high-spirited eight-year-old. Her child is precocious and often rebellious. Victoria's practice of meditation guides her on how best to deal with her child's temperament. She is led to patience and to wisdom. She wants to be a good mother and her guidance tutors her how best to cope.

Sometimes Victoria is strict. At other times she is more lenient, following her cues as she is inwardly guided.

"I depend on guidance," Victoria explains. "Guidance teaches me how to be a good mother. The second half of my day is often difficult. If I wake up early, I'm tired. Guidance helps me to pace myself."

Often tuckered out from her child's hijinks, Victoria enters her evenings craving quiet. But quiet is often not what her child has in mind. As bedtime approaches, she seems to catch a second wind. Victoria finds herself straining to hear guidance.

"'Now what?' I often ask," she relates. This is when her guidance kicks in once again. She has an intuitive thought. *Try reading.* And so, obedient, she coaxes her child to calm down and hear a story. Reading aloud, Victoria finds herself soothed. Her fatigue fades away as she taps an unsuspected inner reservoir of grace.

"Good night, sweetheart," she murmurs to her child. The day's guidance has served her well.

Some things have to be believed to be seen.

—MADELEINE L'ENGLE

JACOB NORDBY IS a genial man. Bearded and muscular, casually dressed, he talks affably and easily about his practice of daily guidance.

"I wake up at peace," he begins. "I rest for a few moments in that liminal space between sleeping and waking, I listen for what bubbles up, perhaps recalling the details of a dream. Then I rouse myself, pad to the door, and let in my cats. I take a few moments to feed them while I brew a cup of coffee. I draw a couple of oracle cards, seeking guidance for the day. Then I settle in to write Morning Pages. After my pages, I go on to meditation. Guidance comes to me through my pages and through my meditation. If I do those two practices, I find that guidance continues to come to me throughout my day."

Jacob pauses, gathering his thoughts. "I can put all this in writing," he volunteers. A gifted writer, he takes readily to the page.

"That would be wonderful," I accept his offer, interested by what further details his writing might uncover.

"I didn't always wake up peaceful," he confesses. "That's just the past few years. Before that, before what might be called my 'spiritual awakening,' I woke up every morning startled."

I try to picture Jacob in his pre-spiritual life. By his own description he was a driven man, working feverishly for success—the house, the car, the job title. Knowing him now, it is difficult to picture him then. Nowadays he is firmly planted on a spiritual path. He seeks guidance and he experiences it.

"I'm alert now for synchronicity," he says. "The other morning I drew the Hummingbird card. Later in the day, looking for a new apartment, I spotted a hummingbird and I thought, 'This is it.'"

Guided by intuition and signs, guided by messages as to his track, Jacob is now a calm and tender man. He lives his life by guidance where he once led his life by blind ambition.

"I believe in prayer," he states softly. He prays for guidance and he receives it. He prays for his own intentions and the intentions of others. I ask him to pray for me when I am going to teach. When the teaching goes well, I phone to thank him.

"Yes," he will say. "I had you in my thoughts that all would go smoothly. I'm glad it did."

Jacob prays when he is asked to pray and he sometimes prays because guidance prompts him to pray.

"What's going on with you?" he may ask. "I felt some agitation this morning so I put you in prayers."

Jacob's guidance is uncanny. When he is prompted to pray, prayers are always needed. His intuition is accurate and, speaking for myself, always welcome.

"Pray for me about my writing," I will sometimes ask him, facing a particularly challenging topic.

Intuition is a sense of knowing how to act spontaneously, without needing to know why.

—SYLVIA CLARE

"Gladly," Jacob replies, and when I write I can feel the booster rocket of his prayers.

Jacob and I sometimes teach together, both of us praying for guidance as to how the course should go. The guidance pays off with the course running smoothly, with each of us by turns leading and following, a nimble duet.

"So, yes," Jacob concludes his thoughts on guidance. "I rely on guidance." Although he doesn't say so, he believes "guidance is where it's at."

The same can be said of James Dybas. A handsome man in his late seventies, he looks far younger. A dancer in his youth, he remains physically fit, priding himself on his fitness routine, which is strenuous. For forty-two years, he has practiced a spiritual path centering on prayer and meditation. Asked if he prays for guidance, he replies, "Yes, but of course. I pray and I meditate. Guidance comes to me chiefly in meditation. I quiet my mind and I receive an instinct about doing something. The pivotal thing is being open to guidance. Clear your mind and get rid of the noises in your head."

James pauses, gathering his thoughts. Then he continues, articulate and eloquent. "The critical thing is the listening part. We all have such busy lives—social media, the news, television, the computer. They all take time and so we must consciously make time to listen. I have a physical practice called Qigong, an ancient Chinese practice. It's very slow. You are moving to take energy from the air, from what's around you. You center yourself. You focus on the now. Guidance comes in the quietness of the moment."

James pauses again, then elaborates on his morning practice. "I read some spiritual literature, twenty minutes of meditation. I pray, 'Guide me. Let me make the right choice based on the information that I have.' I find my instincts are usually right on.

Courage is the most important of all the virtues because without courage, you can't practice any other virtue consistently.

—MAYA ANGELOU

I ask, 'Let me see with clarity and help me to know the next right thing to do.'"

James draws a deep breath, then continues. "I find I make many right choices if I am given the time to sort and clear my mind—to get the noises out of my head. I am also good at homework, at asking, 'What is in the way?' I'm good at culling things necessary to make a proper choice. I find I am guided to the extent I take the time to get quiet. Then, too, you are guided as you have faith that what you are hearing is leading you on the right path."

Pausing yet a third time, James has a concluding thought. "As we get older, the more tools we have, the more faith we have in guidance—which is God consciousness." He adds a footnote. "I hope I've helped."

Your willingness to wrestle with your demons will cause your angels to sing.

—AUGUST WILSON

FOR MORE THAN twenty years, Emma Lively has been a practitioner of Morning Pages. Platinum blond, slender, blue-eyed, she takes to the page while still in her pajamas. She takes seriously the directive that pages must come first, before any of her other morning routines—save coffee. Asked to talk with me about guidance, she is an eager speaker, words tumbling over words as she expresses her thoughts. Guidance is important to her and she practices it a number of ways.

There are the Morning Pages, three pages of longhand morning writing about anything and everything. "I ask questions in Morning Pages and then I listen for an answer. I should probably ask more questions than I do. I ask my question and then I write out the answers. I ask a specific question and I get a specific answer."

Emma pauses, marshaling her thoughts. She continues. "For me, guidance also happens when I'm walking. Sometimes during the day I will take a walk. I'll walk out with a particular question or agenda. It gets answered as I walk. Sometimes I address the question to a specific person. Sometimes it's more general, not to a specific person. Either way, the guidance comes to me."

Emma pauses again, thinking. She goes on, "I've always had intuition. I've always used it. It has been guided and strong. Before I had a name for it, I used it. Later, I got tools, writing out *Q* and *A*. When I am calm, I am often guided. My guidance itself is calm, simple and straightforward, not long-winded."

Emma has a final, important thought. "My guidance is optimistic. I get the strong sense everything is okay, that something is going to work out."

And so for twenty-plus years, Emma has tuned in to guidance. It has given her the conviction that we live in a benevolent world.

We can never obtain peace in the outer world until we make peace with ourselves.

—DALAI LAMA XIV

TALL, SILKEN-HAIRED, SERENE, Laura Leddy depends upon her guidance. Asked to talk about it, she says, "I guess I play my cards close to my chest. This is the first time I've ever talked about guidance."

Catching herself by surprise, she exclaims, "I do get guidance. Oh, I do. It comes to me when I'm calm or when I am occupied with something repetitive—cooking a meal I've cooked many times, chopping vegetables, something routine, when I'm not jabbering in my head."

Laura continues gamely. "I meditate. Have some guided meditations I've done for years. So when I do them, I feel calm and open to the flow. When a message comes, I hear it clearly."

Laura goes onward, exploring her own routines. "I'll look at a photo of my grandparents or remember a loving interaction with them. I'll make a specific request from my grandparents or aunts, someone who has passed on. If I have a question—'tell me what to do about the car'—I give them a spiritual hello and then I ask for guidance."

Laura muses on how guidance comes to her. She explains, "Guidance comes as words or I might get a sudden flash—let's say a wallet, and I'll think, 'Oh, I need to be careful about my spending.' Or let's say it's an image of arts materials. Paints, brushes, canvases. I'll think, 'Oh, I better think of taking up painting again.'

"When I do Morning Pages, I get guidance from them for sure. And I can't say that my guidance has ever been upsetting. It's usually soothing and in line with my own value system. It might not be along the lines I was thinking of, but it's always beneficial."

Laura laughs lightly and confesses, "I occasionally check out online tarot card readings. I may get a good feeling, if not from the full reading, from two or three elements. Then my ears perk up and I think, 'I'm supposed to get that.' It's lighthearted but sometimes it does resonate."

Pausing to collect her impressions, Laura continues, "I do depend on my guidance. Especially if something is causing me mixed feelings. Then I will say, 'I'm looking for clarity.' I ask for it and I get it."

Laura goes on, "For me, guidance is also a part of prayer. When I pray, I get guidance. I don't always know the source, but it comes to me. Heavenly guidance."

Laura goes on thoughtfully, "My surroundings affect me. At certain times of day the light in my apartment is very beautiful. The shadows are lovely. I sit in my recliner and quiet myself. The light is very calming an hour before sunset. I get guidance."

Wrapping up her thoughts, Laura speaks softly. "I pray to my guardian angel to give me guidance, to keep me on track, warn me of things. Sometimes I pray to Mary. When I am sad, oddly, I pray to Jesus. My habits are routines I've developed over a lifetime. I have a book of inspirational quotes. I will open it at random to a message for me. Yes, I must say of all of this: This works."

WRITE FOR GUIDANCE

Who, among your friends, has a spiritual practice you admire? Can you meet for a cup of tea and talk to them about it? Fill in the following:

    1. A person who seems to be guided in their life is . . .

    2. Someone I could speak to about guidance is . . .

    3. If I were brave, I would ask . . .

Now, ask for guidance. What is an action you could take to connect with someone about guidance?

Pleasure is always derived from something outside you, whereas joy arises from within.

—ECKHART TOLLE

GUIDED WORK

It's a hot day but a cooling wind whips through the trees. Nick is over and we decide to brave the heat and walk Lily. Perhaps the wind will cool the day.

Lily is eager for her walk. I take her out most days and she relishes the outings. "Okay, Lily," I carol and she races to the coat rack to retrieve her leash. I snap it to her collar and we set out, Nick leading the way. The courtyard is hot. We scamper across its bricks, climb the stairs to the gate, and take the steps to the dirt road beyond.

"This way, Lily," I cajole her and we head north up a hill. Lily tugs at her leash. We are going too slow. The wind ruffles Lily's coat and tousles our hair. The wind feels good.

"I enjoyed the show," I say to Nick. We have just listened to an hour's podcast between Brian Koppelman and me. Koppelman's questions were smart and far ranging. He has for twenty years been a practitioner of Morning Pages. His enthusiasm for my tool interests and excites me. He cites the pages as being responsible for his colorful and successful career.

"I enjoyed the show, too," Nick echoes me. Koppelman and I recapped the pivotal Artist's Way tools. Nick remarks that the show was well grounded, "useful, I think, to a lot of people."

I worry that perhaps we got a little esoteric, going over a rewriting tool called "green sheets."

"Oh, I think a lot of people will find them useful," Nick assures me.

A lizard crosses our path. Lily darts to the end of her leash. Lizards are, for her, a great delicacy. This one escapes. Lily settles back into trudging, although alert now. Where there was one lizard, there may be more.

"Koppelman was generous to me, praising the book so."

"Yes," Nick concurs. "I loved it when he said to buy ten."

"I love it when I am a building block in someone's dream," I allow.

Now a slow-trudging beetle crosses our path. Lily ignores it. Beetles are not to her taste. A low-flying hummingbird darts overhead. This walk is proving colorful. The road meanders through a patch of juniper trees. Suddenly the air fills with song. Tiny songbirds perch in the trees.

With the new day comes new strength and new thoughts.

—ELEANOR ROOSEVELT

"They're lovely," I remark to Nick, who sighs, "Yes."

What's this? Ahead of us on the road a trio of ravens struts. As we approach them, they linger—taking to the air at the last moment.

"Bold as brass," I say to Nick.

"Yes," he concurs. "We don't scare them."

"I felt well guided during that show," I remark as we circle back, heading toward home.

"Yes. You answered his questions without a pause," Nick tells me. "You were prompt and relaxed."

"I'm afraid he made that easy."

The stiff wind gusts more forcefully. I bow my head and lean into it. Nick does the same. Lily darts to the end of her leash, enjoying the wind.

"I'm glad we listened to the whole show," I volunteer as we walk through my gate.

"Yes. An hour well spent," Nick replies. We one more time scamper across the hot bricks of the courtyard.

"I'm glad we took her out," I announce.

"So am I," Nick replies. "The wind helped, but I'm sure she's appreciative."

"Yes," I say, opening the door. Lily slips inside. Happy for her walk and now to be home. Happy to head for her water bowl.

Watch the stars in their courses as one that runneth about with them therein; and think constantly upon the reciprocal changes of the elements, for thoughts on these things cleanse away the mire of our earthly life.

—MARCUS AURELIUS

At twilight, the mountains loom dark and ominous. Their peaks hulk black against the sky. The moon rises, silver and luminous, dimming the stars. It is witching hour, not day, yet not night. My piñon tree casts shadows, sheltering tiny birds seeking refuge for the night. Inside the house, I flick on lights, settling in to write.

"Can I have guidance for tonight?" I ask the page. *Tonight is a night for writing. We give you thoughts and words,* my guidance responds. I am dubious. I have no thoughts and no words. Not tonight. Instead I feel empty, devoid of inspiration. And so I ask again, "Can I have guidance for tonight?" This time I hear, *Tonight is a night to write. Talk of what's troubling you.* Ah, there's a directive.

Now I have words and thoughts. For two weeks I have been waiting to hear from my British publisher, Andrew Franklin. He has had my prayer book, *Seeking Wisdom,* and I have been waiting to hear his response. Impatient with the wait, I have turned repeatedly to guidance. "What will Andrew think of the book?" I have demanded to know. My guidance has been positive, hopeful, and reassuring. *Andrew is happy with the book,* I've been told. *He will soon make you an offer.*

But "soon" isn't soon enough for me. As each day ticks past, my confidence in my guidance wavers. *Andrew likes the book,* my guidance repeatedly declares, but I harbor dark thoughts. He doesn't like the book, I fear. That's why he's taking so long to get back to me.

Two weeks isn't really very long, my guidance pointedly interjects, but I am not to be comforted. I hold Andrew in the highest regard and his opinion matters to me. Would he like the book? I hope so. My hope is bolstered by facts.

Joel Fotinos, my American editor, "loved" the book and paid a handsome price for it. Susan Raihofer, my literary agent and a tough sell, also "loved" the book. My first tier of readers also *all* "loved" the book. I myself, reading critically, "loved" the book. Surely, I tell myself, Andrew, too, might "love" the book. I am pulling my mood up by my bootstraps. Each long day finds me sinking into paranoia. If he "loved" the book, why isn't he in touch? And yet I know he would be horrified to know of my suffering. He is an advocate of me and my work.

I turn once more to guidance where I am chided for my lack of faith: *Julia, your concerns with Andrew are pointless.*

And so, chided and encouraged, I find myself experiencing a welcome equilibrium. As twilight settles into night, I am, abruptly, hopeful. Perhaps my book is a good one, worthy of the accolades it has been receiving. Perhaps Andrew will get back to me "soon," and "happy with the book." On that positive note, I lay aside my dark thoughts, believing one more time, belatedly, in guidance.

WRITE FOR GUIDANCE

Take pen in hand. Fill in the following:

1. A lingering worry I have about my work is . . .

2. I felt guided when I was working on . . .

3. I would like guidance on . . .

Ask for guidance in any area of your work. Does what you hear surprise you?

GUIDED DECISIONS

Outside my windows, the stiff wind is lashing the trees. The piñon tree shelters tiny birds, safe in its innermost branches. Its outer branches host several ravens, wings flapping in the wind. Inside the house, several—four—large electric fans create a breeze and cool the day's lingering heat. Tomorrow, early, a crew of technicians is due to arrive. They will be installing air conditioning, long overdue and welcome.

"You can afford it," my accountant advised me gravely. "It will add to the value of your house."

"You're sure? It's so expensive!"

"Your teaching monies cover the cost."

"If you're certain—"

"I'm certain." And so the matter was settled.

My East Coast friends were enthusiastic about my plan.

"You'll be so much more comfortable," promised my friend Jeannette.

"You're going to love it," weighed in Emma Lively.

"Can't they come later?" I asked the dispatcher.

"No. I'm afraid not," came back the crisp reply, and so I faced an abbreviated night's sleep and men underfoot for several days.

"Focus on the end result," Jeannette counseled me. "Two or three days' discomfort and a future of ease." As was her habit, Jeannette focused on the positive. "You've been hot, wet, and sweaty," Jeannette went on. "And you've had trouble sleeping. The cool should fix all that."

Focused still on the negative, I called Emma Lively. Maybe she would sympathize. But no.

"It will be over before you know it," Emma optimistically remarked. "You can lock yourself in a different room and write all day."

Listening to her I pictured myself shuttling room to room, notebook in hand. What if I found nothing to write, I wondered.

"I'll call you," Emma promised. So at least I would have company, albeit long distance. Closer at hand, I decided to call my neighbor Scottie Pierce.

"Oh, Scottie, tomorrow I'm having air conditioning installed," I wailed into the phone. Scottie cut me short.

"You're going to love it," she interrupted me. "A couple days' discomfort with workers in your space and then—voila! Cool."

"I have to get up early," I whined.

"I'll tell you what," Scottie interjected. "I'll light incense that it all goes smoothly."

"Oh, Scottie, that would be great," I exclaimed, thinking, just what I needed—prayers!

Upbeat and optimistic, Scottie rang off. Belatedly, I thought of guidance.

"Can I have guidance about the air conditioning?" I queried.

Julia, the workers will be lovely, quiet, and careful, I was told. *You will spend the day writing and it will prove happily productive.*

When you focus on the goodness in your life, you create more of it.

—OPRAH WINFREY

Cornered by my friends and my guidance, I tried to muster some optimism. After all, I told myself, the house had been unbearably hot. The four large fans had made a din—so loud my friend Jennifer refused to talk to me on the phone. "Call me again when it's quiet!" she'd exclaimed. A selling point for the air conditioning was the promise "It's quiet." And so I found myself focusing, as Jeannette advised, on the positive. My house would be cool and quiet, and I myself would be cool and quiet. That's the positive.

It's ironic that on the day air conditioning is being installed, the day is cool and breezy. Maybe I overreacted, I catch myself thinking, forgetting the sweltering days of the week just past. The installation crew arrives, friendly and casual, Cody and Justin. They set to work quickly and efficiently, careful to spread a tarpaulin over my belongings where they work.

"You're an easy job," Cody volunteers to me. "Everything is going smoothly."

By midafternoon, four rooms are prepped. When Nick arrives at three thirty, the workers are already gone for the day. "They're fast," Nick notes appreciatively.

"Yes," I agree. "They are."

Nick gives me a daily computer lesson and I am rapidly learning. Today, to save time, he mans the computer himself, checking my emails. Emails checked and dealt with, I suggest to Nick, "Let's walk Lily. It's cool."

And so we set out with Lily leading the way across the courtyard, through the gate, up the steps to the familiar dirt road where we head, once more, north.

The afternoon is pleasantly cool and a light breeze makes it cooler still. The grove of juniper trees is filled

Everything that slows us down and forces patience, everything that sets us back into the slow circles of nature, is a help.

—MAY SARTON

with songbirds. Their melodies overlap one another and are, as Nick exclaims, "lovely."

The road to the north passes the songbirds and opens out onto a bike trail. We walk the trail with Lily leading the way past chamois bushes, silvery now, gold in autumn.

"How's it going on the guidance book?" Nick asks. A writer himself, he is curious about my progress.

"I'm seventy pages in and have no idea what to write tonight."

"Something will come to you," Nick promises. I pick up the cue.

"Have I asked you about written guidance?" I ask him. He walks a few long steps before he answers, tugging at Lily to slow her pace.

"I do written guidance but I wouldn't say I make it a routine. I tend to take to the page if a question is bothering me, if I don't feel I'm getting enough guidance though the ethers."

"So you go to written guidance for specificity?"

"Yes, but the guidance I get in writing can be very cryptic. I'll think, 'What does that mean?' But then I will go back to it a second time later and I'll think, 'Oh. Now I get it.'"

Nick sidesteps a crack in the trail. He's wearing a new pair of cowboy boots and they can be tricky.

"I find I write three pages and then ask for guidance," I tell him. He snorts in recognition.

"I do that, too," he volunteers. "The writing opens me up to hear guidance."

"So your practice of writing for guidance is pretty casual?" I ask.

"Yes. When I write for guidance I do not capital-*W* write. Instead I try to let go of control of the pen, just seeing what wants to come out."

What if practicing peace is slowing down and realizing there's more to see?

—MORGAN HARPER NICHOLS

"But you'd say you seek written guidance when you need clarity?"

"You could put it that way. Do I make it sound like a last resort?" Nick steps nimbly over another crack in the trail. His new cowboy boots add inches to his height. He turns to face me.

"You use written guidance regularly, don't you?" he demands.

Comparing myself to Nick, I admit, "Yes, I suppose I do."

"Maybe I should try it more," Nick ventures.

"I find it helps," I tell him. "I've been writing for guidance thirty years so it must help."

"Either that or you're stubborn."

"I am stubborn, but it does help." I laugh.

Lily tugs the length of her leash. Our conversation is interesting to us but not to her.

"Home, girl?" I ask her. She knows "home" and that a water bowl awaits her. She sets out at a trot.

trust your heart
if the seas catch fire
(and live by love
though the stars walk
backward)

—E. E. CUMMINGS

THUNDERCLOUDS ARE ROLLING in, down off the mountains. It is monsoon season in Santa Fe and we are told to expect rain every afternoon. I'm hoping that the storms will skip a day. I have holes drilled in my roof at the midpoint of the air conditioning installation.

"It's lovely to work for someone so calm," Cody, the crew's foreman, said to me. I thought, Calm? I'm a nervous wreck, but I guess it doesn't show.

Some beautiful paths
can't be discovered
without getting lost.

—EROL OZAN

Cody's compliment caught me by surprise. All day as the crew hammered and sawed, I'd felt my nerves growing anxious. I called Jeannette for moral support and I walked on the treadmill to expel my nervous energy. Jacob Nordby phoned me to inquire how I was doing. He knew the noise and mess would be disturbing. My little dog Lily responded to the stress in her kingdom by hovering all day close to my ankles. Emma Lively called and warned me to eat despite my anxiety. "You don't need low blood sugar on top of stress," she gravely advised me and so I snuck through the debris to the kitchen where I wolfed down a peanut butter and jelly sandwich.

"By tomorrow you'll be cool," weighed in another caller, Jennifer Bassey. "You're improving your quality of life." Ah, an optimist!

To my daughter, Domenica, I echoed Jennifer's sentiment, "I'm improving my quality of life." But Domenica was not fooled.

"Oh, Mommy, you sound nervous," she observed, accurate across the miles.

"Actually, I am nervous," I confessed. "The noise and the mess . . ." My voice trailed off. I didn't want Domenica to worry. "By this time tomorrow I'll be cool and calm," I advised her.

"How's the puppy?" she asked, not to be deterred from her daughterly job of worrying.

"She's stressed out, too," I admitted. "She's been hovering around my ankles all day."

"Look at it this way," Domenica teased me. "You're improving your quality of life."

Off the phone from Domenica, I received a call from Gerard. "Apart from the mess and din," he said, "how are you handling the installation?"

"I got nervous," I confessed. "Edgy."

"Don't you have a patio you can retreat to?" he asked.

"They were out there, too," I whined.

"Well, after tomorrow, you'll be cool, clean, and quiet," he advised me. "And until tomorrow morning when the crew comes back, enjoy a quiet evening." Gerard's optimism was annoying to me. My nerves were still on edge and what I wanted was sympathy. None forthcoming from Gerard. I got off the phone disgruntled. Optimism be damned.

It was now twilight and the gentle dusk calmed my edgy nerves—dusk and a welcome call from Jeannette. She was brimming with sympathy.

"Given the extent of your disruption, you're doing well," she assured me. "The noise, the mess, your kingdom is overturned. You've done what you can to cope—reaching out to friends, walking on the treadmill. Did you walk Lily? Yes? That's another positive. Bear in mind the end result. The chaos will soon be behind you."

With Jeannette's sympathetic call, I felt my mood shifting. I said to myself, "By tomorrow night it will be over." Lily nuzzled my leg. I thought she understood. Belatedly, I asked for guidance for us both. I heard, *You are doing well. For tonight, set aside your anxiety. Much goodness comes your way.*

As it did so often, my guidance soothed me. Promised goodness was something to look forward to. I padded to the kitchen, placing a casserole in to heat. Dinner as usual told me I was not off kilter any longer. One more time I turned to guidance. This time I heard, *Julia, you are back on track. There is no need for anxiety. All is well.* Listening to the calm advice, I felt the last of my jangled nerves growing still. After all, "much goodness" was to come.

It's easy to make decisions, once you know what your values are.

—ROY O. DISNEY

THE DAY IS hot and hazy. My four fans make noise but do not seem to cool. The air conditioning crew is hard at work. Progress is being made. There is one worker in each of my rooms.

"We're everywhere," exclaims Justin, an affable worker. "It must be hard!"

And it is hard. The workers hammer and saw. My walls sport gaping holes where the air conditioners will fit. Lily is near frantic from the noise. She paces room to room seeking quiet, but there is none.

"It's okay, girl," I croon to her. She looks at me doubtfully, clearly thinking, "*This* is okay?" I coax her to come lie down beside me on the loveseat. My presence spells safety, I hope. Reluctant at first, Lily finally leaps up. She nuzzles my leg, seeking reassurance. "It's okay, girl," I croon again.

The day is an awkward one. My spot on the loveseat is an island of calm amid a sea of chaos. I stroke Lily's silken coat and will her to know just how much I appreciate her company. Working to soothe her, I find myself soothed. Yesterday's nerves belong to yesterday. Today I am able to focus on the forward progress each worker makes. Soon the house will be cool, I tell myself, and in the meanwhile the workers are industrious and sweet-tempered. Things could be far worse.

Cody, the crew's foreman, is sweetly apologetic. He is sorry for the amount of time the work is taking. He promises a fast turnaround on the final day.

"We'll be in and then out," he vows. "It should be a short day."

Cody's apology for taking an extra day goes a long way toward calming my anxiety. I compliment him on the crew's mellow temperament. He smiles and pauses in his work. "That compliment means a lot," he tells me. "We try to hire good crews."

The good crew works long and steadily, draping tarpaulins over my vulnerable belongings. I appreciate their care and the quiet calm with which they work. Rainclouds roll down off the mountains. A clap of thunder rends the air, the only drama in a calm day. Rain pelts the window. A strong wind lashes the piñon tree. Lily hops to the floor, nervous. She hovers by my ankles, seeking safety. Storms frighten her and this storm with its loud peals of thunder is worse than most.

"Did you seal up the condenser?" Justin asks Cody.

"Sure did. I sealed up everything. We shouldn't have any leaks. But this sudden storm came from out of nowhere." Cody

Be settled in your life . . .
in order to be fierce and
original in your work.

—GUSTAVE FLAUBERT

speaks as if chiding the storm for its abrupt appearance. As suddenly as it appeared, the storm vanishes. Cody rounds up his crew.

"We'll see you Monday," he carols to me. "It will take me about another hour in the master bedroom and then another couple hours to finish up the rest."

Cody sounds satisfied. They've done a good day's work, he and his men. They will wrap up with a short final day. I call out a thank-you to the departing crew. I will camp out in my disrupted house over the weekend, and by Monday afternoon the house will be restored to sanity: calm, quiet, and cool.

WRITE FOR GUIDANCE

Is there a pending decision in your life, large or small, that you are trying to make? Write for guidance on this decision. What clarity comes to you?

INVITING CALM

This week will help you to experience the calm of guidance. Guidance brings a sense of serenity and an assurance that we are on the right path. Using the tools of this week, you will be asked to invite the calm of guidance, and, in that calm, examine further self-care in the form of both making connections and setting limits. As the sages say, *Slow equals no.* As you dispense with hurried and harried decision-making, you will find that the pause you experience will forge a deeper connection to a benevolent universe.

GUIDED TO PATIENCE

The day was overcast. Walking Lily, we spotted three lizards. One was fatter and slower than the others and she almost caught it, a delicious mouthful. Tugging at her leash, she darted in pursuit. No luck! The lizard scooted under a rock. Hopes dashed, Lily reluctantly resumed our walk. She was alert for further lizards and two more dashed across our path. Lily lunged after them but they were quick, even quicker than a hungry terrier.

"This way, girl." I tugged on Lily's leash. Obedient but frustrated, she eddied by my side. Lizards, after all, are a delicacy. Our courtyard is an oasis of smooth stones. Lizards bask there in the sunlight, bold and visible. Lily knows their habits and hunts them down as we cross to the courtyard gate. One day she'll catch one. All she needs is patience, but patience is not a terrier's long suit. Nor is it mine. I frequently chide myself, "Patience, Julia," but it is a virtue hard to come by.

In the winter, I wait impatiently for spring. In a cool spring, I yearn for summer. Waiting to hear word from Andrew, I am impatient. Can't he hurry? When I argue with God—and I do—it is most often over timing. I've been waiting six months to hear a good word about my plays and while my guidance swears to me I'll hear *soon*, that "soon" is not soon enough. The seasons move at a temperate pace and theatres match them. Just as I write this, my phone shrills. It is a director calling me to say that she has—finally—heard back from the head of a theatre. The news? Our play—in submission for a Zoom production—has not been read yet. It will get read "soon," we are promised. That word again! And in the meanwhile? Patience.

As I write this, we are in month four of lockdown for the coronavirus. It is July—the end of July—and we have been on lockdown since mid-March. Masks are required. Social distancing is required. Only the most "essential" forays out of our house are allowed. When will it end? Will it soon—or ever—go back to "normal"? To survive these times a virtue is required. Yes. Patience.

Patience is what Job needed. Patience is what all of us require now. It takes patience not to inquire, "When, God?" Meaning, "Please, God, *now*." We are, all of us, globally, being tutored in patience. As we don our masks, scrub our already clean hands, make our brief "essential" trips into the world, we are learning to be patient. Waiting in line for entrance to a grocery or pharmacy, we are being taught, yes, patience.

I am, by nature, impatient. Weekends loom long for me. I can't wait for Monday, for the world to be back at work. Surely Monday I will hear from Andrew. I have spent the weekend writing him imaginary emails, demanding, "So! What did you think?" But protocol requires that I wait for him to contact my literary agent who will then contact me with the—hopefully—good news of his approval and offer. My guidance has told me that his offer will be "modest" but very welcome. I am ready to accept a modest offer—any offer—if only word of it will come.

On Sunday afternoon, officially a day of rest, I emailed my

We don't realize that, somewhere within us all, there does exist a supreme Self who is eternally at peace.

—ELIZABETH GILBERT

agent who was spending quality time with her family. I wrote, "Can you think of anything that we can do to shake the tree?" As I expected, I did not hear back from her. One more time I was being asked for patience. And, in any case, I knew what she would say: "Waiting is hard. Patience!"

Chided, I took to the page, hoping guidance would have wisdom to share. I asked, "How can I find patience?" I heard, *Call Emma. She is good at patience. She worked six years on her musical. You can wait six days more on Andrew.*

The guidance at first made me furious, but then it drew things to scale. Chastened, I realized I could wait, if not patiently, impatiently. But wait I would because, however difficult, I could.

I want to beg you . . . to be patient toward all that is unsolved in your heart. . . . Live the questions now.

—RAINER MARIA RILKE

THE NIGHT SKY WAS both silver and gold. The setting sun gilded the mountaintops. I was settled in to write when my phone rang. The caller was my friend Jennifer Bassey, who wanted to give me a talking-to about patience.

"So you haven't heard from Andrew?" she asked.

"No," I said, sounding miserable.

"He's going to like the book," she promised. "If he doesn't, I'll jump off my balcony. Actually, I won't, but you get my drift."

"And my air conditioning crew didn't show up," I wailed.

"Not at all?"

"Not at all."

"Well, they must have had a crisis. That happens with workmen."

"They say they are coming tomorrow at eight thirty A.M."

"So you just need patience. Patience with Andrew, patience with your crew. I know how it is with you—as with me. We want what we want when we want it and that's *now*. Try to accept that they are on God's timetable, not yours. Take a deep breath. Relax. Everything will happen when it's supposed to happen."

"Ah, Jennifer, I try to have patience." Did I sound as impatient as I felt? I hate being lectured to, no matter how well meaning. But Jennifer had more to say.

"Call two people and ask them about *them,*" she gravely advised me.

"I know that works," I responded, thinking, Please, no more lectures on patience. I don't have the patience!

Jennifer may have sensed my unspoken resistance because she abruptly got off the phone. Against my better judgment, I decided to take her advice, phoning my friend Julianna, fellow writer.

"Hello, sweetheart," Julianna gaily caroled. "What do you hear from London?"

"Radio silence. Nothing yet."

"Rats. I've been praying and praying."

Julianna sounded as impatient as I felt. She exclaimed, "I *loved* the book!" Mentally, I added her name to my list of "loved its." If I valued Andrew's opinion and couldn't wait to hear it, I treasured Julianna's verdict. I felt my cup tipping: half-full, not half-empty. Julianna's opinion held as much weight with me as Andrew's. I had a reprieve from anxiety. If she thought the book was good, perhaps it was good. Gratefully, I got off the phone. Moments later, following Jennifer's advice, I phoned Jacob Nordby.

"How are you?" I remembered to ask him before launching into my tale of woe.

"I just took a walk by the river and it was lovely," Jacob responded. "Now I'm home and settling in for the night. Have you had any word from Andrew, your publisher?"

"Radio silence," I reported. "It's been nearly two weeks. As every day ticks past, I fall further into paranoia."

"What does your guidance say?" Jacob asked. He believed in the accuracy of my guidance as surely as he believed in the accuracy of his own.

Have love for your inner Self and everything else is done for you.

—AMIT RAY

"Guidance tells me my worries about Andrew are pointless," I answered. I could quote the optimism of guidance even if I couldn't believe it.

"He'll like the book," Jacob predicted cheerfully. "It's a good book. I loved it."

Now, after both Julianna and Jacob weighed in, I found myself less anxious. Could all my readers be wrong? I doubted it. Andrew had only to go alone with the consensus. But would he? He was very much his own man.

The evening sky darkened into night. The silvery moon rose over the mountains. Buoyed by the support of my friends, I dressed for bed. I'd endured one more day of waiting. Perhaps tomorrow I would hear from Andrew. Until then, I needed to keep the faith.

I WOKE UP early, preparing to meet my air conditioner crew. Installation had dragged on five days and I was impatient that the work be over and done with. They arrived on schedule, early for a workday, and I perched on my loveseat, out of their way. I was tired after my short night's sleep and so I drank three full mugs of coffee, fighting to wake up. My Morning Pages took a long time. My fatigue slowed my pen. I was on page three, the finale, when my phone rang. It was Emma Lively, brimming with news.

"You've heard from Andrew," she blurted. "He wants to publish the book. Susan Raihofer emailed me his email in case I talked to you before she did. Shall I read you what he wrote?"

"Yes, please! I'm dying to hear."

Emma took a swig of water and cleared her throat. She read: "I have been reading and found myself riveted. It is not a natural book for me. I am both a Jew and an atheist and I think those categories are not your target audience. Despite those facts, I am

I can't help hoping, and keeping faith, and loving beauty.

—T. H. WHITE

For [the river] knew now where it was going, and it said to itself, "There is no hurry. We shall get there some day."

—A. A. MILNE

finding the book appealing, touching, and personally relevant. That surprised me. I thought I would read the book, discover the audience, and understand the purpose the book served. But it goes beyond that. It speaks to me personally. That is the power of your writing. So, we will definitely be making an offer."

"Oh, Emma, that's wonderful!" I exclaimed. "Read it to me again!"

And so Emma read me Andrew's notes a second time. I found myself marveling at his open-mindedness: "I am both a Jew and an atheist." That he, a non-believer, could embrace my believer's book struck me as near miraculous. What did he mean the book was "personally relevant"? Perhaps he would tell me when next we talked. He was, after all, the publisher of *The Artist's Way,* subtitled *A Spiritual Path to Higher Creativity.* Did he believe in the power of a higher power, a creative energy, that he chose not to call "God"? He was, I knew, an avid gardener. To me nature spoke of God while perhaps to him it spoke of creative energy, no deity needed.

Getting off the phone from a jubilant Emma, I phoned an equally jubilant Susan Raihofer. As my agent, she, like me, had waited for Andrew's response. Now, like me, she was exuberant. She bottom-lined the response: "He's going to make an offer. He put it in writing!"

But now it was my turn to put something in writing. I emailed Andrew: "I don't think you can know how much I count on your opinion. You are a muse and an ally." Sending my note across the Atlantic, I felt a sense of elation. I wanted him to know how much I valued him.

The day sped past. I phoned my friend Julianna to tell her the good news. She was thrilled for me. I phoned Nick and Jacob and Scottie and Laura and Jeannette and Jennifer. One and all, they were excited for me. I was excited myself, so excited I almost didn't care when Cody, the foreman of the crew, told me they were having difficulties with the system. A special technician would need to be called in. He couldn't come today. He would come tomorrow.

"Yes," Cody said. "He will troubleshoot the system. A solution will be found." All I needed would be that dreaded word "patience."

I heard him out and took him at his word. "A solution will be found." In the meanwhile, I counted my blessings. A delay in the air conditioning was just that—a delay. By far of more importance was the delay that had ended. Andrew loved the book.

WRITE FOR GUIDANCE

Choose an area in your life where you are struggling to have patience. Write out the following questions, and listen for your guidance.

1. What do I need to know?
2. What do I need to do?
3. What do I need to grieve?
4. What do I need to accept?
5. What do I need to celebrate?

ACCEPTING GOOD

My house is cool. Air conditioning has been installed successfully. When the technician arrived early this morning, it took him all of five minutes to locate the glitch—an error in the wiring, easily fixed. Eager to be on his way to his next job, he gave me a very brief tutorial on how to run the system. I listened carefully, trying not to be overwhelmed. I am spooked by all things technical and the air conditioning smacked to me of difficulty. True, I would be cool, but would I be too cool? How precisely to adjust the temperature? My grasp of gadgetry was minimal. My little dog stretched out in bliss in the newly cool living room. I tried stretching out myself.

Silvery clouds descend from the mountains. It is twilight. Evening is upon us. In the west, the setting sun streaks the sky with multicolored light. In the east, the moon is rising. My living room is cool and dim. I flick on the lights. Little Lily pads to my side. "Up, girl," I urge her and after a moment's hesitation, she leaps to the loveseat, settling in by my side. We are a cozy duo.

Nick came to work with me this afternoon. Stepping inside from the sweltering heat, he exclaimed, "Ah, this is refreshing." The newly installed air conditioning was doing its job.

"Do you like it?" Nick asked.

"Yes, I'm getting used to it," I answered.

Now, with Lily by my side, I find myself relishing the cool. My hair is no longer damp with sweat. My clothes no longer cling to my body. Accustomed to discomfort, I find the comfort of the cool startling. I have joined the modern age. My hand, moving across the page, is cool. For that matter, the page itself is cool. Moment by moment I find myself at ease. When my phone shrills, I hesitate to answer it. I am so enjoying the calm.

But I do answer the phone and the caller is Jennifer. Herself enjoying air conditioning in hot and humid South Florida, she is like Nick, anxious that I like my new cool.

"Are they all done?" Jennifer asks. "It took them forever. Do you like it? You must. You were suffering so from the heat."

"I think I like it," I tell her. "But it takes some getting used to."

"Yes, but do you like it?" she demands to know.

"Lily likes it," I tell her. I think of my little dog stretched out on the loveseat, stretched out on the cool tiles.

"I'll bet she does," Jennifer replies.

"After all," I joke, "she wears a fur coat."

Satisfied that I am modern and comfortable, Jennifer rings off. Immediately, the phone shrills again. This time, my caller is my friend Scottie. I fill her in on the drama at my house: the new cool.

He that can have Patience, can have what he will.

—BENJAMIN FRANKLIN

IT IS A day later—an eventful day, busy. I walked on the treadmill, worked out with my trainer, walked little Lily, worked

Why is patience so important? Because it makes us pay attention.

—PAULO COELHO

on belated correspondence, did a forty-five-minute podcast on which I read four of my poems. It's evening now, a full-moon night, but the moon is blocked by rain clouds hovering over the mountains. I'm curled on my loveseat. Lily is curled beside me. One more time, heavy raindrops pelt the windows, although this time there is neither thunder nor lightning. The raindrops *ping* but that is all.

My day was a day of nerves and adrenaline. My physical energy outstripped my spiritual energy.

"I'm nervous," I told both Scottie and Jennifer. "Pray for me!" Both friends said they would gladly pray and so I engaged the podcast feeling bolstered. The host was a young poet and she made me—and my poetry—feel welcome. I selected four poems from my album *This Earth*. She received them gleefully. "Please read more," she said after the first poem. I read three more.

"A treat," she pronounced them.

Little did she know that her "treat" was a treat for me. I enjoyed bringing out my poet, exhibiting the artist behind *The Artist's Way*. Reading my poetry to an acknowledged poet took nerve—or courage. After all, she made her life as a poet. I made poetry of my life. And yet, due to her generosity, we met as peers, two poets, writing. She shared that her audience, both international and national, had just completed *The Artist's Way*. I shared from my creativity toolkit tools I thought particularly relevant to writers. The time of the podcast flew by and we parted as newly found friends.

"Thank you, Scottie," I phone now to say. "It went well."

"But did you have fun?" she asks.

"Yes, actually, I did. I shared some of my poetry."

"Aha. That must have been fun."

"It was. I felt seen as an artist."

"Well, you are an artist."

"Thank you. It was fun to be 'out.'"

"Well, my dear friend, I'm glad it went well. I had the incense burning!" Scottie chuckles, happy with her answered prayer. We end our call.

Next I telephone Jennifer. She answers my call with a question.

"Hello, sweetheart. How did it go?"

"Well," I tell her. "Very well."

"That's the power of prayer," she replies. "When I have an audition, I will ask God to work through me. Watching the tape later, I will see something special in my performance. 'That's God,' I will say. 'I never would have thought of that.' My performance was God's."

"I read four poems," I report.

"The inspiration to do that came from God," Jennifer says with certainty. "You've never done that before, have you?"

"No."

"Then it was God. When I have an audition—or a job—I say, 'God, you do it. I might screw it up.'"

"I didn't screw it up."

"Then you need to say, 'Thank you, God.'"

I tell Jennifer I am filled with gratitude.

"Tell God," she scolds me. And so, getting off our call, I pray, "Thank you, God, for giving me courage." Is it my imagination that I hear: *You're welcome.*

There's no advantage to hurrying through life.

—MASASHI KISHIMOTO

JUANITA NAVA COMES to my house every Monday afternoon. For three hours she scrubs and vacuums and dusts. She is a whirlwind of energy. She leaves my house spotless, sparkling. Her mood is unfailingly gay and sweet-tempered. Her presence in the house brings both order and joy. She is a hard worker and a festive one. In her evening hours, she teaches dance. Why is she always so happy? I wonder. This afternoon, I asked.

"I pray all the time," Juanita answered me. "I pray in the morning, at night before bed, and all through the day. When I'm driving job to job, I pray. I don't pray formal prayers, I pray as I talk. It's casual, a conversation, talking to God."

Juanita is petite with a dancer's compact build. She is lean and muscular, fit and energetic. Her prayer life is the key to her energy and stamina. She told me that.

"I have a connection," she told me, pausing in her work to focus on my question. She didn't find it intrusive. Rather, she was delighted to share her source of cheer and guidance: regular, daily prayer.

"I grew up praying," she told me next. "I taught my own children to pray and believe."

I thought to myself that Juanita's children are, like their mother, beacons of good cheer. Her two teenaged boys are happy-go-lucky and well-mannered. They are, again, like their mother, hardworking and enjoyable.

"I'm glad you asked me your question," Juanita said now. "You pray, don't you?"

"I do," I answered.

Juanita prayed for guidance to do the next right thing. She cleaned my house, moving swiftly and easily task to task to task, prayer to prayer to prayer.

"Sometimes," she told me, "I wake up in the middle of the night and I pray, then I fall back asleep. I wake up in the morning and I pray again."

By the time Juanita arrives at my house midafternoon, she has already put in a full day's prayers. Her guidance leads her in her work. Every week she finds something new to tackle. This week she cleared spiderwebs from an outside window. Just how she managed it, I don't know. I do know that Lily shadowed her as she worked, attracted, doubtless, by her good cheer and the fact that she has three dogs at home and is a self-declared dog lover.

"You need trash bags, laundry detergent, dish detergent, and coffee filters," Juanita declared to me at her work's end. "I'll bring them to you next week."

Grateful for her help, I found myself praying—praying a prayer of gratitude. "Thank you, God, for bringing me Juanita." She left for the day with a sweet goodbye.

"Until next Monday, Julia."

"Until then, Juanita. Thank you!"

WRITE FOR GUIDANCE

Fill in the following:

1. An area in my life where I accept good is . . .
2. I could accept more good in my life by . . .
3. My guidance led me to good when . . .

Let things flow naturally forward in whatever way they like.

—VERNON HOWARD

THE CALM OF GUIDANCE

The sky is lit apricot and silver. The colors contrast but complement each other. The setting sun donates the apricot. The encroaching evening brings on the silver. My living room is cool and dim once again. Once again I flick on the lights and settle in to write. I've had a day of guidance—hunches, intuitions, answered prayers. Walking Lily, I was struck anew by the beauty all around me: juniper trees filled with songbirds, mountain vistas with towering heights, thunderheads looming steep and majestic, a cooling wind gracing all.

I walked with Nick. We matched strides with Lily trotting ahead the length of her leash.

"You're happy," Nick observed.

"I had a good day so far," I told him.

"You're grounded," he remarked. "Calm. At ease."

"Thank you," I answered, adding, "Walking with you and Lily helps."

Lily skidded to a halt. She tiptoed forward to where a tiny songbird lay on the road.

"Here, Lily," I coaxed her, tugging at her leash.

"Poor little bird," Nick crooned.

The tiny bird was blue and gold. Perhaps a finch. It might have flown into a car, knocking its fragile life from its body.

"Poor little bird," Nick repeated.

"This way, girl," I chided Lily. Reluctantly, Lily abandoned her treasure.

The sight of the little bird saddened me. I once kept a pair of lovebirds, colored like the tiny finch. My house is a veritable gallery of Audubon prints. Like my father, a birder, I am fond of winged things.

"What did you do about the podcast you were uncomfortable with?" Nick asked me.

"I turned it down," I told him. "It was too crazy. A five-minute segment for 'five hot tips from the creativity expert.' It smacked of sound bites to me. I just wasn't comfortable."

"As long as you're happy. I think you need to trust your intuition."

"Well, I ran it by guidance and got told I was correct to cancel."

"And so you trusted your guidance?"

"Yes. It has quite a track record."

Lily pulled to the side of the road, sniffing. She was on the trail of something—another dog, a raccoon, a lizard, a deer?

"This way, girl," I coaxed, tugging at her leash to show I meant business. "Lily, I mean it," I scolded her. She relinquished her hunt. Approaching our gate, she suddenly plunged ahead: a lizard! A lizard! Lily was quick but the lizard was quicker. It scooted under a rock under a cactus. Lily was foiled. We descended the steps to the garden. Last night it had hosted a cottontail. Now there was none to be seen.

"It's going to be a lovely evening," Nick mused. The cool breeze stirred my birch trees.

"Yes," I agreed, thinking of my friend Jennifer under a

You are the sky. Everything else—it's just the weather.

—PEMA CHÖDRÖN

*Forcing a project to
completion,
you ruin what was
almost ripe.*

—LAO TZU

hurricane watch in South Florida. Slipping into the newly cool house, I dashed to answer a ringing phone. It was Jennifer.

"It passed us by," she exclaimed breathlessly. "It's been downgraded to a tropical storm. I just wanted you to know we are safe. We may be in for a couple days of torrential rains but that's all."

I thanked Jennifer for reporting in. Nick unsnapped Lily's leash and hung it on the coatrack.

"Until tomorrow?" he asked.

"Until tomorrow," I answered. I walked him to the door, opening it out onto the courtyard.

"Have a peaceful and cool evening," Nick wished me.

"Thank you, Nick. I will."

THUNDERHEADS BILLOW OVER the mountains. Closer in, the sky is blue. The piñon tree stirs in the wind. Weather is on the way. I sit quietly, seeking guidance. I have prayed "for me and my beloveds." The aftermath of prayer is calm. In the calm comes guidance. *Call Scottie,* I hear.

My friend Scottie sits quietly every day at dawn. She reads, she prays, she chants, and then she simply sits, burning sticks of incense, sending her intentions to the heavens. Her two small dogs, Jackson and Moxie, know to sit quietly, joining her in meditation. Theirs is a peaceful household. I know that, later in the day, when I call her and ask how she is, her reply will be, "Julia, I'm excellent." Her steady equilibrium is the fruit of her quiet time. Guided daily by her inner compass, she moves smoothly through her days. She is surefooted in her interactions. Her "luck" is steady, a direct result of guidance.

"I'm led," Scottie says simply. She is led and she obediently follows. Her faith is strong and her actions are as well. When she is guided, she listens. Listening, she intuits a path. She takes that path a step at a time. In the evening, she sits quiet a second time, reviewing her day, asking further guidance if any.

Scottie's calm assurance draws things to scale. I picture her in her calm abode, quietly lighting a stick of incense.

"My house faces east," she explained to me once. "It's dark when I get up, but then the sun rises as I sit. It's an auspicious time." Lighting her incense, sitting calm, Scottie greets the day. Each day is blessed by her quiet time. Each day unfolds as she asks, "with ease and joy."

Seeking ease and joy, I call Scottie. Her house is down the mountain from my house and with the change in altitude our weather often differs. Just now the sky at my altitude is spitting rain. At Scottie's altitude there is rain mixed with hail. She croons to her dogs as I do to mine. We want them to feel safe but at both altitudes there is thunder and lightning—scary for dogs. Lily retreats to a hiding place, the corner behind my coatrack. Scottie's two dogs hover near her side.

"I'm going to put the boys to bed," Scottie tells me.

"Lily's hiding," I volunteer. "I've got the jitters, too, although the storm up here isn't much of a storm."

"The boys are nervous. So let me call you later," Scottie asks. We hang up the phone.

A half hour passes uneventfully. The storm is over. Scottie rings me again.

"I've been thinking," she says. "Have you written guidance? I'm thinking it would comfort you. You have such a strong connection. What about writing to your two deceased friends, Jane and Elberta? I think it would comfort you to hear from them, to have a nice chat. I think you need to realize that your guidance has your back, supporting you at every turn."

Scottie pauses for breath, then she continues, "Your guidance is strong and accurate. Go to your guidance for reassurance." Scottie's voice is firm. She knows what I should do.

I live in the faith that there is a Presence and Power greater than I am that nurtures and supports me in ways I could not even imagine. I know that this Presence is All knowing and All Power and is Always right where I am.

—ERNEST HOLMES

Support and encouragement are found in the most unlikely places.

—RAQUEL CEPEDA

"I'll try it," I tell her. Once again we hang up the phone. I settle in on the loveseat, taking pen to page.

"Can I hear from Jane?" I ask. I hear: *Julia, I am at your side. You have no need for fear. The higher power provides for you and you will be well cared for. You always have a choice: faith or fear. You can choose faith, knowing that you are always cared for. Trust.*

Jane speaks as she spoke in life. Her voice and message are familiar and comforting. I ask next: "Can I hear from Elberta?" *Julia, you are a champion. I give you grace and stamina. You are on track and doing well. It's good to hear from you.*

Scottie was right. Guidance feels reassuring. While I wrote, the storm clouds passed. The moon has risen over the mountains and a clear evening prevails. Lily creeps from her hiding place and sits sentinel on the deck. All is calm.

WRITE FOR GUIDANCE

Our guidance is calming. As we habitually write for guidance, our decisions are made with more ease, and we move through the world with more calm.

Fill in the following:

1. My guidance calmed me when . . .
2. A decision I made based on guidance was . . .
3. I saw my guidance as a source of steadiness in my life when . . .

Now, choose a person who is deceased whose guidance you find calming. Can you reach out to them on the page, and listen for the response?

THE SUPPORT OF CONNECTION

I spent yesterday evening with John and Chris Kukulski, a happily married couple. Chris made dinner for the three of us, seated at opposite ends of a long plank table. John poured three goblets of iced tea, peach or plain. The delicious main course was chicken pad Thai, a savory dish liberally sprinkled with red chili pepper.

"Do you like green chiles?" Chris, the chef, asked me.

"I do."

"Well, our garden has quite a batch coming along and we'll give you some."

"That would be fantastic," I said eagerly.

"And do you like tomatoes?" John asked. "We have a bumper crop."

Vegetables, delicious vegetables, anchored one end of the Kukulski garden. Flowers, brilliant and abundant, anchored the other.

"See how the cosmos are coming!" Chris exclaimed. "I spend

an hour or two on the garden every morning." His diligence showed as blossoms tumbled over blossoms seeking, by their nature, sun or shade.

"He cooks for an army," John announced fondly. "I'm not an army."

Towering well over six feet, Chris smiled down at his diminutive spouse. John is a full foot shorter than his mate.

"Seconds?" Chris asked, ladling himself a generous portion.

John and I demurred. One serving was plenty.

"We have a little light dessert—mango or raspberry sorbet," John offered.

"I'll take raspberry," I said.

"Raspberry for me, too," Chris volunteered, spearing a last morsel of chicken.

"Mango for me," John chimed in as he scooped the sorbet into tiny, fluted bowls.

From the master bedroom came a plaintive *meow*. It was the voice of Simon, their young cat, begging to be allowed to mingle.

"He's very social," Chris explained. "And you are our first guest since lockdown. He's wondering, 'Who is that lady?'"

Who indeed?

John, Chris, and I share a spiritual path. I have pursued it for decades. They are in their early years but we are all agreed on the necessity of guidance. We each have a favored prayer but one, the serenity prayer, is used by us all. "God, grant me the serenity to accept the things I cannot change, the courage to change the things I can, and the wisdom to know the difference."

Chris prays by gardening, reveling in the out of doors. John prays by keeping an immaculate house, a hundred-year-old adobe filled with antiques. I pray, as they both know, by writing. We are all agreed on the value of prayer.

"Let me give you some tomatoes," John offered as our quiet

evening wore down. And so he gave me a bag of tomatoes while Chris promised once more that there would soon be green chiles.

"Thank you, you two," I bade them good night. Driving home as the sun was setting, I spotted a doe—a beautiful, graceful animal trotting along the roadside. A perfect ending to a perfect evening.

A WEEK HAS passed—an eventful week. My newly installed air conditioning broke and I spent several nights sleeping to the roar of a fan, not really cool but not unbearably hot. The unbearable heat came during the day and I waited days for the air conditioners to be fixed. At first, predictably, the technicians blamed me for the breakdown. I had set the controls wrong, they told me. They set them "right" and, just as they were leaving, the units stopped again. This was a challenge. They set about testing the system and, climbing to the roof, they discovered four separate leaks, to their chagrin. Working all day—nearly eight full hours—they repaired the leaks and set the system up again. One of the technicians, a tall, lanky man named Josh, took me aside.

"You didn't do anything wrong," he assured me. "The leaks were the result of hurried work by the installation crew." So I breathed a long sigh of relief. "The system should work perfectly now," he continued. "And you know how to find me if you have any trouble."

Josh left and the system continued to function. I turned my attention to another problem—mice! I found a dead mouse on my kitchen floor and then I found another. Anthony, my wizardly handyman, explained.

"They're eating the poison I set out for them," he reported. "That's why you're finding them in the middle of the floor. Leave on the kitchen lights and close the dog door. Put the dog food in the refrigerator overnight."

The best mirror is an old friend.

—GEORGE HERBERT

"Anthony," I said, "would you be insulted if I hired an exterminator? Could you find me one?"

"I'll get on it," Anthony answered. "My feelings are not hurt."

Relieved but jittery—mice!—I left the lights blazing in the kitchen and called Lily inside so I could close the dog door after her. She was used to eating in the night so I apologized as I put her food in the refrigerator. Lily is bright but my antics baffled her. All this over mice?

Anthony called me early the next morning. "I found an exterminator for you. Here's his name and number. He's expecting your call."

Eager, I took down the name and number. I called and a firm and friendly voice answered. "This is Julia Cameron," I said. "Anthony called you about me?"

"Yes, he did. He filled me in on all he's tried. What if I come by this afternoon? We'll walk the property."

And so, although the prospect of walking the property looking for mice frightened me, I set a time. That done, I called Nick and asked if he could walk the property for me. He said he could. Next up I had a call from Juanita. She, too, said she would talk to the exterminator, Gustavo.

At five fifteen, the designated hour, Gustavo, Nick, and Juanita rendezvoused. They walked the property, then came indoors where Gustavo promptly found four entryways for the mice—behind the stove, under the sink, under the bathroom sink, behind the washing machine. Juanita corroborated that these were trouble spots. Gustavo advised me, as Anthony had, to leave lights blazing and dog door shut, the food put away in the refrigerator. He would be back on Monday, armed with supplies and ready to mouse-safe the premises. He named a modest price. "But pay me after I've done the work."

I thanked Gustavo, thanked Juanita, thanked Nick, and after

they left, I called to thank Anthony. "He's efficient and ethical. Thank you," I told him.

"Yes," said Anthony. "He's a good guy."

"You're a good guy," I told him. "Thank you."

WRITE FOR GUIDANCE

We have practiced the art of finding support through our guidance. Now, it is time to actively connect with those around us. Is there an area in which you need human support? Is there a friend you can reach out to, just for connection?

Ask your guidance what human connection or support would best serve you at this time. Can you make a plan to connect?

A friend may be waiting behind a stranger's face.

—MAYA ANGELOU

SETTING BOUNDARIES

With my house in order, I could finally turn my attention back to the page. I found clarity had been given to me in my week's absence. A troublesome interview I had conducted for this book suddenly seemed exactly that: "troublesome." Rather than trying one more time to fix it, I decided on a clearer, more radical move: the interview should be cut. Taking pen in hand, I found the offending pages—and I boldly X-ed them out. Now my book was mine once again. The air conditioning, the mice, and the book were all problems solved.

My friend Scottie called. I told her of my decision to cut the interview. "Good for you," she affirmed. "He's an arrogant, pretentious, self-serving man. You—and your book—deserved better." Validated by Scottie, relieved of pests of all types, I settled into the cool of my living room. I asked for guidance and was promptly told: *You are correct to cut him from the book. He is arrogant and wants more credit than he is due.* I thought of mailing him a dead mouse.

* * *

IT'S NEARLY TIME for my daily check-in with Jeannette. Like Scottie, she is glad that I cut the offending interview. I read her the humorous poem I wrote to give me the "courage of my evictions." It ends:

AND SO AT LAST HIS TALE IS CUT.
THERE IS NO PLACE FOR SUCH A NUT.

"That's excellent!" she exclaims. And her chuckle warms the wire.

"I had a hard time until I wrote the poem," I tell her. "And now I have a poem about my air conditioning, too":

THEY PROMISED COOL AND CALM AND QUIET
INSTEAD THEIR WORK IS BAD—JUST TRY IT.

With two little poems to my credit, I explain, "If I can be funny, I get my power back."

"Yes," says Jeannette, "I can see that." I read her the entry about mailing a dead mouse. She laughs again. I feel myself bonding with her more deeply. Our shared laughter lingers in the air.

"You liked the little poems."

"Oh yes. And I do think that humor gives back power. Maybe now you'll be able to write freely."

"I hope so. I've had a full week of pests and toxins."

"What does your guidance say?"

I recite:

LITTLE ONE, YOU'RE DOING WELL
YOUR HOUSE HAS BEEN A LIVING HELL.

Be in your own skin, as an act of self-loving.

—H. RAVEN ROSE

In the universe, there are things that are known, and things that are unknown, and in between them, there are doors.

—WILLIAM BLAKE

"True!" Jeannette crows. "I detect a breakthrough!"

And so I ask her, "You trust my guidance, don't you?"

"Oh, absolutely," she replies. "What did it tell you tonight?"

I page back to the evening's guidance. I read it aloud. "*We are on track and sharp. You are going to write well and we are proud of you.*"

"Can you let that soak in?" Jeannette asks.

"Not yet," I tell her. But already a little poem is forming.

THIS LITTLE POEM GOES OUT TO MY MICE
I'LL KILL YOU DEAD NOT ONCE BUT TWICE!

And a moment later I have another ditty.

THIS LITTLE POEM IS THANKS TO MY FRIENDS
A HAPPY ENDING IS HOW THIS TALE ENDS.

I think of Scottie and Jeannette both tickled by my naughtiness. I think of Jennifer and Emma both rooting for me during my block. Humor unlocks the lock, I rhyme again. And then,

THIS LITTLE HOUSE DESERVES A POEM
RHYMING MAKES A HOUSE A HOME.

I turn one more time to my guidance. I read: *There is no error in your path.* I add, "The many troubles caused your wrath."

"Can you accept your anger?" Jeannette asks.

"Now that I've written it out—I shout!"

AND SO THIS ENTRY DRAWS TO A CLOSE
I'VE VENTED ANGER, HEAVEN KNOWS!

WRITE FOR GUIDANCE

I have long believed in the power of writing silly poems to help "right" my energies. Fill in the following:

1. A person who has been bothering me is . . .
2. I wish I could . . .
3. My guidance suggests . . .

Now, write a silly poem "at" the person or situation. Does it shift your mood, and draw your energies back into yourself?

We can think of anger as a sentry, stalking the edges of our boundaries and standing ready to defend them.

—JESSICA MOORE

INVITING OPTIMISM

This week you will use guidance to consciously invite optimism into your life. You will explore areas where you can find self-forgiveness and a sense of hope. By this point in the course, guidance is likely coming more and more easily to you. It is my hope that you are experiencing its steadiness and coming to trust and rely on it. You will also try using guidance in relation to your creative projects, as artists have done for centuries. Counting your positives—the things you did right—helps you build a grounded and optimistic sense of self. You are not powerless. You have many small choice points where you can spot the good. For example, "I ate well today." "I walked." "I maintained my emotional equilibrium during a difficult conversation." "I used my strength gently, saying what I mean—but not saying it mean."

GUIDED TO
SELF-FORGIVENESS

Your need is gentleness, the guidance read. *Write tonight on self-forgiveness. You will be led.*

I read the guidance over. I definitely needed gentleness. I was beating myself up over my shortcomings. I had spent the afternoon "visiting" a book club and the "visit" had proved a difficult one. The club was reported to be thirty people, all working through my book *The Artist's Way*. When I arrived (via Zoom) I found a mere handful of people. We "visited" for an hour with the questions from the participants few and far between. The moderator stepped into the void with questions that were far afield from my book. I answered the scattered questions as well as I was able, hoping to be helpful. I found myself being gentle with the little group, hoping to coax them forward. The visit ended on a positive note and I found myself—suddenly—spiraling downward.

"What didn't I say?" my inner critic demanded, and there followed a list of could-haves and should-haves. I tried, in vain,

Faith requires following the power of a whisper.

—SHANNON L. ALDER

When I stopped to take a breath, I noticed I had wings.

—JODI LIVON

to think of what I might have done right. Instead I encountered a list of negatives. I wasn't smart, humorous, charismatic. Instead I was— What was I? The answer came zooming from my depths: "Not good enough."

I called my friend Emma Lively. She had attended the book club.

"Emma," I said, "I feel terrible."

"Julia," she said, "you did fine. You said a lot of gentle, encouraging things. I wrote some of them down. They struck me as so wise."

Boosted by Emma's encouragement, I asked to hear what I'd said. Emma read me her list of quotes. I was astonished—my words were kind, gentle, encouraging, even inspirational. They were, I realized, more than good enough. I had hoped to be clever and my words were something better. They were useful. I had asked my friends to pray for me and their prayers had rendered me of service. It was, I realized, my ego that felt out of joint. My ego demanded of me that I be perfect. By "perfect" I meant "brilliant." But "brilliant" was not what was called for. "Useful" was.

WRITE FOR GUIDANCE

Fill in the following:

1. I wish I could be more gentle with myself about . . .

2. I can't seem to forgive myself for . . .

Now, addressing your guidance, write out the following questions, and then listen for a response:

1. How can I be more gentle with myself?

2. How can I have more self-forgiveness?

GUIDED TO HOPE

I woke to a bright new day. The sun was shining. The dark mood of yesterday was banished.

"What shall I write about?" I queried guidance. The answer came back: *Write about hope.*

The topic struck me as knife-edged. After all, just yesterday I had been hopeless. My friend Nick came to the rescue.

"What do you think about hope?" I asked him.

Nick drew a deep breath, then he announced, "Hope is critical. It is the bedrock for prayer. You hope—and pray—that a situation will open up. Oh, there are days when I feel hopeless, like your day yesterday, when I cannot pray, but those days pass as hope is restored."

"So," I said, "hope is essential. Hope and faith."

"Yes. Look how much better you feel today than yesterday." Nick had a point, but just then Lily leapt up for his attention. She had hope that he would take her for a walk.

"In a minute, girl," Nick crooned, retrieving her leash from its resting place. Lily leapt up again, wriggling with excitement.

How wonderful it is that nobody need wait a single moment before starting to improve the world.

—ANNE FRANK

*Write it on your heart
that every day is the best
day in the year.*

—RALPH WALDO
EMERSON

Nick successfully snapped on her leash. The three of us set out on a walk, turning north up the dirt road where Lily hopefully hunted for lizards. She spotted two but they darted in opposite directions and she was foiled.

Passing the juniper grove, birdsong filled the air. I matched my stride to Nick's and he hurried to keep abreast of Lily, who was sniffing eagerly at the roadside, hoping for more lizards.

"This way, girl," Nick said firmly, tugging at her leash to establish his leadership. Reluctantly, Lily eddied to his side. Her lizard-hunting hopes were dashed only to return again as we headed back toward home.

"She has hope," I joked to Nick. He kept a close hold on her leash. I thought back to the day that Lily had cornered a lizard. Was it so delicious a mouthful that she was ever hopeful of another? Nick shepherded her to the door. I thanked him for his company and retreated with Lily into the cool of the house. My phone was ringing. I answered happily. The caller was Jeannette.

"Jeannette," I answered breathlessly. "What do you think about hope?"

"It's essential," Jeannette responded. "It's the unspoken force that keeps you going. If I didn't believe in hope there would be no point to prayer."

I knew Jeannette believed in the power of prayer. "Go on," I urged her.

"You can't pray without hope. If you didn't think something would come of it, there would be no reason to pray. Think of it. You're striving on a path and you're hoping something will be different. You hope—and trust—that something will be better."

"I know you pray in the morning," I told her. "But do you pray at night?"

"I pray at night for help with anxiety. I say one word over and over. Help, mercy, peace. Help is a popular one-word prayer. I say one word and ask to let it go."

"Do you pray on your knees?" I pried.

"I don't get down on my knees, not since I was little. I pray when shopping, washing dishes, brushing teeth, cleaning. At night I pray hoping—there's that word again—hoping for a better tomorrow."

"You pray for me at night? For me to have a better tomorrow?"

"Oh, yes."

"Well, last night's prayers were answered. I had a better today."

"I hoped you would," Jeannette said, signing off—"and I prayed."

WRITE FOR GUIDANCE

We all have hope. One of the quickest ways to tune into our own hope—and its power—is to turn to this tool. Take pen in hand, and, writing as quickly as you can, fill in the following:

1. I hope . . .
2. I hope . . .
3. I hope . . .
4. I hope . . .
5. I hope . . .
6. I hope . . .
7. I hope . . .
8. I hope . . .
9. I hope . . .
10. I hope . . .

Even the darkest night
will end
And the sun will rise.

—HERBERT KRETZMER

SURRENDERING CONTROL

The mountains to the north and east are blocked by smoke. A forest fire is blazing. The air at my house, twenty miles away, is filled with ash. If I step outside and take a deep breath, my lungs sting. The beautiful little village of Tesuque lies in the path of the fire and a woman I know, Marisa, lives in an isolated house at close range. I am hoping for the best for her. It's terrifying enough at my hopefully safe remove. I think of the fires that blazed last year in California, the homes and lives destroyed. By comparison our fire is little—so far—and may soon be safely contained. For Marisa's sake, I hope so.

The distant fire arouses primordial fear. The smoke-filled air creates anxiety. As twilight nears, the wind shifts, and the mountains become visible. The sky to the west—away from the fire—is molten gold. A fireball sun sinks below the horizon.

"What should I write about?" I ask the page. I want to hear guidance but my thoughts are on the fire and no words come to me. And then I hear, *Your need is prayer. Your help comes to you from many sources.* I phone my new friend Susan who lives in California. "I'm grumpy and petty," I tell her. I do not mention the fire. She, after all, is from California where fires are *fires.*

"You're allowed to have a grumpy day," she tells me. Her voice holds a warm chuckle and years of experience on a spiritual path.

"I hate feeling petty," I tell her. Then I launch into a recital of things on my nerves—people who are self-centered—the way I myself am feeling. I still do not mention the fire and the fact that the smoky air has my nerves frayed. Susan says she understands having people on my nerves. We agree to talk tomorrow when I will hopefully be in better spirits. But what if the fire crawls closer in the night?

MORNING BRINGS WITH it a smoke-filled wind. The mountains loom only as shadows. The ash-laden air speaks of the fire's stubborn continuance. I call Marisa, checking on her safety.

"It's still two miles away," she reported, her voice hoarse from the wind's debris. "The wind is shifting, carrying the fire away from me. I'm going to be all right."

True to Marisa's report, the wind is shifting. The mountains come into focus, spared from catastrophe.

"The fire is soon to be contained," Nick phones to tell me. "The wind is blowing north and west. No structures in Tesuque have fallen prey."

Looking out my large window, I see the evidence of Nick's report. The smoke is thinning over the little village of Tesuque. It gathered to the west, over uninhabited land. My little dog Lily ventures out to the deck. The smoke no longer stings her eyes. She rests happily in a patch of sunlight. When I call her in, she comes reluctantly. I promised her a walk. Yesterday, with the smoke and heat, I kept her confined. Now I snap her leash to

Part of being optimistic is keeping one's head pointed toward the sun, one's feet moving forward.

—NELSON MANDELA

*I am so far from being
a pessimist. . . . On the
contrary, in spite of my
scars, I am tickled to
death at life.*

—EUGENE O'NEILL

her collar and together we set out. The temperature is still hovering near ninety, but Marisa's wind sweeps down, cooling our path. Lily is alert for lizards but there are none to be seen. The smoky wind of the morning has driven them all to seek cover. Frustrated, Lily trots ahead of me. I tug at her leash—"Slow down"—our walk, after all, is pleasant. The wind blows her coat.

Back at the house, the phone is ringing. The caller is Laura, concerned about the fire. From her apartment in Chicago, the news of a forest fire was dramatic.

"Laura," I tell her, "it's moving away."

"But have they contained it?" she presses.

"They say soon," I tell her. "The air is much cleaner. I took Lily out for a walk."

News of my dog walk seems to reassure her.

"I've got you in prayers," she volunteers. "For safety."

I thank her for her prayers. From faraway Chicago I feel her goodwill.

Lily laps at her water bowl, slaking her ticklish thirst. I get a bottle of cold water from the refrigerator. Drinking it, I think, Although it's better, there's still smoke in the air. The mountains loom dark at twilight. Perhaps tomorrow they will be clear.

ANOTHER DAY, GRAY and heavy. The fire is a continuing saga: the mountains are shadows of themselves. Smoke-laden winds blot out their peaks. Rain threatens but doesn't fall. The fire is still not contained. My piñon tree is etched dark green against a glowering gray sky. Tiny birds shelter in its verdant arms. Walking Lily past a juniper grove, I hear no birdsong. The smoky air has stifled the songbirds. Perhaps it scratched their tiny throats.

Twilight descends on the mountains as one more shade of

gray. The sunset is muted. The rainclouds glide by, carrying their cargo of water away from the fire. More rain for later in the week is predicted but we need it now. The fire burns on with the rainclouds a tease as they pass from sight.

My house is at a safe remove from the fire. There is a ridge of high mountains standing guard. As long as the winds hold steady to the north and west, I have no cause for concern. But the smoky air stifles me like the songbirds. I try to write but words escape me. I want to print a single word: FIRE!

THE ASH-SOAKED AIR obscures the mountains. Walking Lily, my eyes sting and my lungs burn. It is perhaps foolish to venture out. Lily coughs—a delicate cough—and I think of the animals fleeing the fire. For many of them, their homes are destroyed. Their safety is threatened and they flee from the flames. Firefighters spot deer and bear. The first fleet-footed; the second lumbering, united in their peril. I cut short Lily's walk, shepherding her back to the house where a bowl of cold water will sooth her ticklish throat.

I look out my large window to the dimly outlined mountains. The fire burns on and sorrow is carried on the wind. When the rain finally falls, it will be as though the sky is weeping. So much waste—a fallen forest. Green turned to black, a shroud on the earth. Grief hangs in the air.

Speaking for myself, I am melancholy. All day long, my mood has been blue. "It's in the air," Nick announces. He, too, is blue. "There's nothing I can pin it on," he tells me, but Nick is a sensitive soul and his grief for the wildlife is deep, as is mine. Nick checks hourly for news of the fire. "Eighteen percent contained," he reports to me, hoping for better news.

As twilight falls, Lily hovers near my side. Peals of thunder

In this hour I do not believe that any darkness will endure!

—J. R. R. TOLKIEN

Anything can happen,
  child,
ANYTHING can be.

  —SHEL SILVERSTEIN

speak of rain, but no rain falls. No one has said how the fire started. A careless campfire? It doesn't really matter. However it started, the blaze took off. At first a small fire, then a larger, now a big fire. Not, perhaps, compared to California fires, but big enough to scare us in Santa Fe.

As the thunder rumbles on and no rain falls, Lily moans softly, pacing the floor. The aborted storm is unnatural and she is nervous.

"It's okay, girl," I tell her, but she is unconvinced. And who can blame her? The rumble of thunder turns to a roar. Still no rain. Now I am joining Lily in her nerves. "It's okay," I tell us both. Looking past my piñon tree to the east and north, no mountains are visible. Smoke cloaks their heights. Behind its veil, the fire licks hungrily. Acres fall prey to its appetite. The promised rain would slow its spread but the rain doesn't fall.

And now the thunder mutes its voice. The storm has passed us by.

Lily leaps to the loveseat by my side. She licks my hand. If she could write, she would tell us to have peace. The wind is shifting and the mountains are once again visible, hulking silver against the sky. The moon rises, obscured by shifting smoke. The stars are dimmed.

My phone shrills. The caller is Scott Thomas. He tells me that the rain which skipped my area fell heavily on his. "We had thunder and lightning and rain," he relates the storm. My melancholia lifts at his news. I can hope the fire is quenched.

WRITE FOR GUIDANCE

Fill in the following:

  1. An area in my life where I have no control is . . .
  2. I wish that . . .
  3. I am afraid that . . .

Now, write out the following questions and listen for guidance. What do you hear?

1. How can I accept my lack of control?
2. How can I turn this situation over to a higher power?
3. What action can I take?

Choose to be optimistic,
it feels better.

—DALAI LAMA XIV

RELIANCE ON GUIDANCE

It's ninety degrees and smoky in Santa Fe. It's sixty-five and crystal clear in Northern Michigan where my friend, artist Ezra Hubbard, is summering.

"Hello, you," Ezra says when he reaches me. "I had a dream of you the other night and I took it as a signal—call."

Ezra is dressed in summer gear—a navy blue polo shirt, khaki shorts, green shoes. He has gone for a long bike ride, the better to gather his thoughts, and now he calls me prepared to talk about guidance.

"I get up at six A.M.," he starts off. "I have an alarm clock that gives off light, not sound, and I'm up before the sun is. I sit on the edge of my bed doing some deep-breathing exercises and then I'm up to coffee and the page."

Ezra pauses, collecting his thoughts. "I write Morning Pages first thing, sitting in my studio or out on the porch. I sit still and listen. Maybe I recall dreams or parts of dreams. I get them on the page. I write three pages, gathering my thoughts, and then I write an extra page of everything I hope to accomplish in my day, even down to the time I will do it."

Ezra pauses again, wanting to be accurate, then he continues. "I write, and then after I write, I sketch. I draw pictures of pieces I've made and of pieces I'm going to make, a sort of visual record of my ongoing work. This takes me about an hour and a half. It makes for me a feedback loop. I see the sculptures I have made and I try out new designs. At day's end, I review what I've done. I check it against the list of what I hoped to accomplish."

Ezra clears his throat. The conversation is, for him, emotional. "I trust my guidance because I have to. Sometimes I doubt when I'm not hearing much advice but then I stomp around and the guidance comes back. Reviewing my day, I see what I have learned."

From where Ezra sits, he has a view of tall trees and Lake Michigan beyond. Close at hand there is a single apple tree with slowly reddening fruit.

"I believe I'm led," Ezra speaks on. "Sometimes the guidance is confusing but in hindsight, it always makes sense. Each piece I make has a message embedded in it, right down to the form and line. Yes, there are messages in the work—absolutely. Sometimes it's a conversation with a person or with what you might call the 'spirit' of the piece."

The best way to not feel hopeless is to get up and do something.

—BARACK OBAMA

I tell Ezra that I have a piece of his across the room from me as we talk. It is a round disc of wood bisected by a cross. Its message is spiritual yet grounded. In the years that I have owned it, the piece has never ceased to talk to me.

"Yes!" Ezra exclaims, excited to have his work validated. I tell him that his sculpture brings me peace and joy.

"I take long bike rides to clear my thinking," Ezra adds thoughtfully. "It works like running. I get a sense of direction."

*Remember that hope is
a good thing . . . maybe
the best of things, and no
good thing ever dies.*

—STEPHEN KING

Ezra plucks at his belt. His shorts hang loosely on his lanky frame. He makes a steeple with his hands, then spreads them, palms up.

"Here in Michigan I have the time and space to create, but I miss the company of other artists. They are available to me on Zoom, but it's not the same. It's a mixed bag. The isolation gives me space to work but I'd have to say it's lonely."

With daily pages and solitary bike rides, Ezra is his own witness. He sums it up: "I trust guidance because I have to."

THE FIRE IS not quenched but it is better. Instead of a full smoky sky, there is a single plume of smoke. The rain that did not fall at my house did fall on the fire. It was a drizzle, not a downpour, but it helped.

The clearer skies were cause for optimism. The fire would, eventually, pass. More rain is predicted. Tonight I watch the evening sky and the mountains stand out in bas-relief. Instead of a veil of smoke, there are individual clouds. The sunset glows in the west—topaz as it illumines the last remaining smoke.

I have been teaching four decades, since I was thirty-two. I'm now seventy-two and I have long years of practice behind me. Each class is individual, and each class requires prayer. I ask to be guided in what and how I teach and—guided—I stand before rooms of people listening, always, for the hunch or intuition on how to proceed.

I like to take to the page before a class. I ask for love, service, humor, wisdom, and, yes—charisma. I ask for specific guidance on precisely how to proceed. Today, writing for guidance, I was told, *Open the class with poetry and song.* I am a poet and a composer, but it wouldn't have occurred to me to bring my poetry and music in to play. Over the years I have learned to be obedient, to follow the guidance however far-fetched it may seem. And so, this afternoon, I opened my class with a poem, "Why We Write." I liked stepping out from behind my teaching persona again and revealing myself as an artist, the artist who wrote *The Artist's Way.*

Teaching, the guidance comes to me not as a voice but an impulse. *Do this next.* And so I *do* do "this" next. *Sing,* the guidance nudged me today, and so I sang, a cappella, a small song I had written. *You will lead by example,* my written guidance had advised me before the class and so I found myself teaching boldly, sharing stories from my own writer's experience.

You will need to be vulnerable, I was further advised, and I found myself telling the class that after forty books, I still suffer the feeling that I am an imposter, not a *real* writer, whatever that means. I told them about my inner critic, whom I call Nigel. Nigel is a British interior decorator and nothing that I write meets his lofty standards. I've been writing since I was eighteen and Nigel's naysaying has accompanied me every step of the way. "Thank you for sharing, Nigel," I have learned to counter his volleys of negativity. Accomplished artists have learned to create in the face of fear, not because they are fearless. I have written entire books with Nigel hissing in my ear. "Thank you for sharing, Nigel," I have learned to retort. And so, leading by example, vulnerable as directed, I model for the class creating despite fear.

My classes are an hour and a half and the ninety minutes leaves me feeling exultant and exhausted. I closed today's class with another poem and I admired the tidiness of my guidance.

Creativity takes courage.

—HENRI MATISSE

WRITE FOR GUIDANCE

There are times when it takes much more strength to know when to let go and then do it.

—ANN LANDERS

Fill in the following:

1. An area in my life where I must rely on guidance is . . .
2. A time when my guidance proved to be reliable was . . .
3. I suspect I can trust my guidance on this issue because . . .

THE STEADINESS OF GUIDANCE

The mountains are etched sharply against the sky. Billowing white clouds crown their heights. Above the clouds, the sky is an azure bowl. Pinprick stars stud its darkening expanse. The evening is tranquil. Perched on my loveseat, looking out my bay window, I am struck by nature's calm. The drama of the fire is past.

Write about steadiness, my guidance advises me, and I reach within my psyche for a calm center. Where is it? I am still disturbed by the fire and the emotions it provoked. I love my house and I felt it to be in jeopardy. The smoky wind carried danger and I felt it. I depended on Nick to keep me abreast of the fire's progress and direction. He, at least, was calm.

"It's heading away from you. You have nothing to fear," he advised me gravely, intuiting the anxiety hidden by my calm voice. "The wind is blowing north and west," he assured me. "Your house lies to the south and east."

Nick's reassurance gave me something to cling to. As the

For after all, the best
thing one can do
When it is raining, is to
let it rain.

—HENRY WADSWORTH
LONGFELLOW

Unfold your own myth.

—RUMI

smoke cleared from the sky, I prayed a prayer of gratitude. "Thank you," I breathed at my bedside. "Thank you." My windows showed me a vista of the sky and mountains. As the air cleared, the mountains loomed high and familiar.

My spiritual path assures me that all is—always—well. *You are safe and protected,* my guidance assures me. *All is well.* The calming words soothe me. I repeat, as a mantra, "All is well."

But it takes faith to rest in guidance. My jagged nerves need faith. I reach out one more time to the Great Creator. I am told, firmly, *The earth will heal.* I look out my windows to the north and, lo, there is no plume of smoke. Rain is predicted for later in the night and the scorched earth will cool. Clouds of steam will rise from the ashes. Moisture will drench the fallen forest. From the ashes, new growth will come.

"All is well," I tell myself, watching as a crescent moon blesses the sky. It is the moon of new beginnings. "All is well," the new moon tells me. I believe it.

I'M LYING IN bed—lazy—when the phone shrills. I glance at caller ID and am delighted to rouse myself. The caller is my friend Ed Towle, a close friend for forty-two years. I picture him tall and lanky, blond-haired, bearded, with a ready smile creasing his features. He is returning my call to him of last night when I decided I needed a dose of his good humor. When times are dark, Ed remains lighthearted. His is a determined optimism. He cultivates a sunny mood, laughing easily, chuckling at life's vagaries. Now he says, "I want to sleep until this pandemic is over." He isn't sleeping. He's calling me. "Are you up and about?" he asks.

"Getting there," I answer.

"So what are you up to? Writing?"

"I'm writing a book on guidance."

"Aha. That's a hard topic. You will need guidance to write about guidance. Do you bowl?"

"I have."

"Well, you know when children bowl, we put inflatable bumpers in the gutters; the ball can't fall in. That's what guidance is like—bumpers to keep us on track."

Ed's image is a happy one. I picture inflatable bumpers steering his course and mine.

"Do you pray for guidance?" I ask him, picturing him on his knees with a balloon-like bumper tucked under each arm, holding him steady, while he phrases his petition.

"I don't call it 'prayer,'" he responds. "Though in fact it is. I don't go to church. The back yard will do. Any quiet place. I sit with my issue and my mind bumps along, fast and noisy. Then, after a bit, I feel my mind growing quiet, smooth and slow. That's when guidance comes. I feel my mind going to a smoother, quieter flow. The speedy, noisy mind is off to the side. Guidance comes to me then. I know what to do."

Ed's is a tranquil life. His reliance upon guidance is casual and organic. When troubled, he simply takes himself to the quiet of his back yard. Settled there, he sits calmly, waiting for his mind to slow and clear. The question that disturbed him comes into focus: as he waits, the answer replaces the question.

"It's simple, really," he sums up his experience. He asks for guidance and it comes. No big deal, but something he depends on.

WRITE FOR GUIDANCE

Writing for guidance, we find a calm center. We can also consciously take ourselves to a calm location—a park, a garden, a church or synagogue—to tap into a larger calm around us.

Imagination is more important than knowledge. Knowledge is limited. Imagination encircles the world.

—ALBERT EINSTEIN

Take your notebook and pen to a place you find calm. Ask for guidance about whatever is pressing, and listen for the response. Does the environment enhance your ability to hear your guidance?

GUIDANCE AND ART

Brendan Constantine is a poet—a noted poet—and he is an eloquent and articulate speaker. Shaved-headed since 1997, with piercing blue eyes, he is a striking figure in a plaid shirt, blue jeans, canary-yellow socks, and dark shoes. He wears his reading glasses, the better to focus his remarks. He speaks swiftly and eagerly, glad to be of service.

"My prayers are not formal. They're very conversational. I don't understand what God is—the force that made molecules and meteors and mountains—but I speak to it frankly, sometimes full-voiced, sometimes in a whisper. I speak to God first thing on waking. I talk as to someone right next to me, an intimate. I ask to be useful. I use that word. And so my day begins."

Brendan takes a deep breath and then plunges onward. "What I have manifested as an artist is closely bound to my spiritual life. My desire to be useful—and an attitude of acceptance—enables my art. Another word for it is 'astonishment.' A dialogue with everything throughout my day. My conversation with a higher power on how the universe is going. Throughout the day

All great achievements of science must start from intuitive knowledge. I believe in intuition and inspiration. . . . At times I feel certain I am right while not knowing the reason.

—ALBERT EINSTEIN

We're curious . . . and curiosity keeps leading us down new paths.

—WALT DISNEY

I'm blessed with just enough sight to move forward toward the horizon. As though something is saying, *'Keep going, keep coming, just a little further.'* That is guidance and I follow guidance."

Brendan leans forward, eager to be clear. "I will say that having had a rich experience of guidance, I can sometimes look for it too hard. I get caught on self-consciousness. No matter how connected I may feel, I'm still the same flawed human being."

Brendan sighs. His tone is confessional. "I do experience guidance in my writing. Sometimes it feels like the poem already exists in some ether, that it is an entity with whom I am negotiating rather than creating. . . . There are other times when I am painfully aware that I am bringing something into being and it feels like an act of will on my part. My guidance may be asking for help. Sometimes from another person."

Brendan clears his throat, aware that he is talking with great velocity. He rushes onward. "My guidance is something I seek to do what I'm supposed to, to practice my art well. And yet, I'm a believer in making mistakes because error may be the form the guidance takes. Some lessons can only be learned that way."

Brendan's is the voice of experience. He has been writing full-time since 1994 and he has learned his craft by trial and error. "I have come away sometimes thinking, 'Wow. I hope I never do that again.'"

And yet overall, the arc of his art has been positive. "I have been working in earnest two and a half decades, and in that time my guidance and art have become how I think, how I pray. How I make sense of the world. I'm listening for guidance every step of the way."

WRITE FOR GUIDANCE

What creative project are you working on? Have you tried asking for guidance about it?

INVITING STAMINA

This week, you will be encouraged to stay the course, and to turn to guidance even as you revisit issues or anxieties that have plagued you in the past. The tools of this week aim to remind you that guidance is always available to us, and always a source of support. The practice of writing out guidance yields us a steady and useful life. As we learned last week, counting our positives gives us a sense of spiritual muscle. We face old challenges with new strength.

NATURE'S MAGIC

Nick and I walk Lily in the cool of the evening. Summer's heat is dropping away and fall hovers at the threshold. The mountains are green and purple and soon they will turn gold as the aspen pass into their most glorious season. Last year, fall was brief as an early and harsh winter settled in. This year I am hoping for a respite. Soon the chamisa bushes will flare gold and the summer's lizards will disappear. It is bear season. The magnificent animals lumber down from the heights, thrusting themselves near human habitats until autumn passes and they retreat to hibernate once again.

"Bear alert" the word passes through my area. And so I am cautious making my way through the courtyard and into my house.

"Deer alert" might better be said as the elegant animals pick their way from the mountains to the valley floor, nibbling the grasses as they go. After the summer, they are fat and sleek. Winter will find them leaner as they forage a less verdant domain.

My garden is host to some unwelcome creatures: moles are

If I have the belief that I can do it, I shall surely acquire the capacity to do it even if I may not have it at the beginning.

—MAHATMA GANDHI

burrowing beneath the rose bushes. Walking out, Lily tugs at her leash, eager to have at them. "No, girl," I say, restraining her and her appetite. She is disappointed to be so foiled.

My property is a wooded acre. Piñon trees and juniper perch cheek to jowl. Tonight, with a full moon rising, the trees are more silver than black. The moonlight illumines Lily's dog yard—half an acre, carefully fenced. Lily ventures out, scouting her enclosure for intruders. A posse of coyotes skirts the fence. Lily barks at them and they howl, singing their threat. They cannot scale the fence and Lily knows it. She stands her ground, yelping a warning for the intruders to clear out. It is a standoff. Neither Lily nor the coyotes give ground.

"Lily, treats!" I carol, luring her inside. I close the dog door, trapping her indoors. The coyotes are, to me, too close for comfort.

The full moon washes the courtyard silver. A few hardy rose-bushes bloom despite the moles. I talked to an exterminator about the moles and learned that trapping them was an expensive and elaborate procedure. And so I decided to let them have their way.

I'm curled on the couch, writing, when the phone shrills. The caller is Scott Thomas, who reports that his house has visitors—three raccoons balancing in the branches of the elm tree that shades his patio. His pit bull announced the intruders' arrival, barking at the door, begging to be let out and to have at them.

"I've seen bigger," Scott tells me. "These must be adolescents. They only come at night and they are fearless. When I shine my flashlight on them, they just stare back. Do you get any?"

"No," I answer. "I don't think they like my trees."

"Well, my dog doesn't like them. It's his house and he resents them."

"I get coyotes," I volunteer. "And Lily doesn't like them."

"No, of course not."

"I know she's safe in her yard but I bring her in."

"Better safe than sorry. It's wise to bring her in."

On that cautionary note, Scott signs off. Lily leaps to the back of the loveseat and stares out the window. She is alert for more intruders.

"It's okay, girl," I tell her, but I myself am staring out the window. The full moon illuminates my domain. I watch for creatures great and small. Perhaps tonight I'll have raccoons. I find I hope so.

IT'S LATE AFTERNOON and the heat is waning. Earlier—hotter— Nick and I walked Lily. Tiny lizards darted across our path. Lily ignored them. Mature lizards are more to her taste. The pavement was hot and I was on the lookout for snakes—red racers and bull snakes outnumber rattlers at my altitude. Nick has no fear of snakes. "They're our friends," he proclaims. "Bull snakes eat mice." And so, I should welcome them. Mice are an ever-present presence. The friendly snakes trim the population. However friendly, I'm still scared of them. And so on my walks with Lily and Nick I am hypervigilant, but lizards are the only creatures that I spy and lizards, oddly, do not frighten me.

I had my house exterminated for mice and the exterminator, a kindly man, sympathized with my fear of snakes. "You don't need to worry. They won't come in the house," he advised me, pinpointing my apprehension that one might slide in the dog door. "They're shy and they avoid people and people's habitats," he continued. "You really have nothing to worry about."

I didn't tell him the source of my fear. A friend had regaled me with a tale of a huge snake climbing onto the deck at his house to eat a baby bird. My portal hosted a nest of baby birds. Did that mean it would attract a predatory snake? Perhaps a bull snake with an appetite for more than mice? I worried.

Lily scampered gaily down the courtyard steps. The stones

But I know, somehow, that only when it is dark enough, can you see the stars.

—MARTIN LUTHER KING, JR.

on either side of the stairs harbored many lizards. She was ready to pounce but the lizards were too quick for her. Still, hope sprang eternal and Lily was ever hopeful. Nick tugged at her leash and she reluctantly gave up the hunt. Tiny songbirds caroled our arrival home. They sang until sunset and then with the dimming day, they grew hushed. At twilight, ravens took to the sky, searching out their nocturnal perch. In contrast to the songbirds' lilting melodies, they cawed raucously, teasing Lily down below. Lily looked to the sky ready to do battle. The ravens challenged her, nearly her size. Their mocking calls teased her and so I said to Nick, "Let's bring her in."

Stubborn, Lily braced her legs. She wasn't ready for her adventure to end. "Come on, girl," I coaxed, and she relented. Threading her way in the door, she headed for her water bowl. The afternoon's antics had left her thirsty. Her tags jangled against the bowl as she drank. Thirst quenched, she leapt to the back of the loveseat, staring out the window to the adventures she'd left behind.

THE MOUNTAINS ARE golden. The aspen have turned from green to vivid gold. Tomorrow I will make the steep drive up curving roads, speed limit ten miles per hour, to view their glory firsthand. The aspen groves are like giant flames reaching to the sky. My visit won't be long. Even a few minutes in their fiery glow is enough. The aspen season is short. I have learned to go to them quickly. Delay a few days and their radiance will have passed.

Tonight a stiff breeze stirs my piñon tree. Groves of piñon climb the slopes to the aspen trees. Like their showier golden sisters, they are beautiful. Nick professes to love them more—perhaps because they are bountiful. Their cargo of tiny nuts feeds the birds. My own piñon tree is abundant. It feeds songbirds and ravens alike.

Last year was a bumper crop. "Can I harvest your piñon?"

Anthony asked. Given the go-ahead, he filled buckets. "I'll roast you some nuts," he volunteered. The birds eat them raw. The squirrels feast on their leftovers.

Tonight the moon is half-full. Its champagne glass of radiance lights the mountain peaks. The phone shrills and it is my daughter. She has had a flurry of birthday phone calls and they cheered her greatly. "A day early but I loved them!" she crows. She also reports receiving a notecard from me. I wrote her how proud I am of her as a wife and mother. She is tickled by the praise.

I tell her that I spent the afternoon teaching, three hundred people, on Zoom. It was a difficult class and I judged myself to have been "adequate." Emma and Nick, who both attended the class, declared my performance "fine, really excellent." I take their votes to heart and try to bolster my mood. That is when I notice that the aspen are aglow. Their beauty lifts my heart and I plot tomorrow's visitation. I will take little Lily with me, tutoring her in autumn's beauty.

To stop dreaming—well, that's like saying you can never change your fate.

—AMY TAN

WRITE FOR GUIDANCE

I find that bringing nature into my home—in the form of fresh-cut flowers, or collected pinecones, or a blooming plant—helps me connect with the divine. Can you bring an element of nature into your home? Does it give you a sense of awe and connection to nature's innate magic?

Gardening is an instrument of grace.

—MAY SARTON

ALLOWING DIVINE SUPPORT

This is true of any and all of the natural laws; they have always existed, and as soon as understood may be used.

—ERNEST HOLMES

Today I taught a Zoom class of 183 people. The subject? Prayer. The class title, "Talking to God." I was nervous before I taught—I am always nervous before I teach. I prayed, "Help me to help my class, to give them what they need." After a difficult class yesterday, I was worried that I would fail. Prayer, after all, is a difficult subject and I approached teaching it with trepidation. "Give me ease and relaxation," I petitioned God. I asked additionally for a list of qualities I wanted to embody: love, wisdom, usefulness, good humor, charisma, connection, compassion, stamina, energy, eloquence. . . . I prayed, "Dear God, I confess I want to be brilliant. Help me, please, to be satisfied with what I am able to do."

And so, armed with multiple wishes, I opened the class. "Let's count to three and then set an intention for the class to go well. One, two, three . . ." I felt the good energy of the students' intentions. I launched into teaching feeling relaxed and at ease, an answered prayer. For the next ninety minutes I taught, moving from point to point, tool to tool. I felt myself being guided: *Do this next, say that.* I closed the class with the serenity prayer: "God, grant me the serenity to accept the things I cannot change, courage to change the things I can, and wisdom to know the difference."

I had asked to be satisfied with what I was able to do and I found myself with an answered prayer. I felt no regrets. The class had been good.

The clearest way into the Universe is through a forest wilderness.

—JOHN MUIR

"DEAR GOD, PLEASE give me words," I prayed tonight. Then I listened. I needed a flow of words to capture tonight's topic: control. I had closed the class with a prayer about control. The serenity prayer is a prayer of sorting what we can control and what we cannot. Using it, we relinquish control. Instead we ask God to be the one in charge, to "grant" us wisdom as we face our perplexities. We let go of our preconceived notions, our illusions of control. We recognize that we are in fact powerless over people, places, and things. Our difficulties arise out of our attempts at control. Our will becomes an agenda as we strive for desired outcomes. Sometimes the world cooperates with our intention, and that invites the delusion that we have power. Often, however, the world fails to yield to our desires and we become frustrated. Where is our control?

We have no control. In dealing with people there is always the uncomfortable fact of free will. The one we love may love another and all of our wishes to the contrary don't change the dismal facts.

Events, too, seem to have a will of their own. We wish for a certain outcome. We will it with all our hearts and—lo!—the outcome differs from our desires. Events fall into place without regard for our preferences. Free will may one more time be at play as people behave contrary to our wishes, putting into motion events beyond our control.

What happens? Our will is thwarted. One more time we

are out of control. Denied our wishes, we become angry, even vengeful. We struggle against circumstances, hoping for a change. When no change comes, we are exhausted.

All of us, at times, have the illusion of control. People and events go our way and we wax victorious. But then what happens? A gear slips and we spin out of control. All efforts of our will fail to change the day. We would do well to surrender to the flow of events, but surrender doesn't come easily. Instead, we struggle, caught in the grip of events beyond our power to change.

Our beloved loves another. Our investment proves unwise. We're struck by a health crisis. An accident befalls us. All of these are beyond our control. Is there no escape?

Escape lies in surrender. In going along with events as they unfold. Sober alcoholics turn their "will and their lives" over to the care of a higher power. They seek to align their will with God's. When events run counter to their wishes, they remind themselves that they've made a deal: God is in charge. For civilians this is a radical but effective stance. As they surrender to fate, goodness comes to play. Grace enters the scene. They see that their attempts at control are futile and so they strive for acceptance. And acceptance is the key to being comfortable out of control.

I wonder if the snow loves the trees and fields, that it kisses them so gently? And then it covers them up snug, you know, with a white quilt; and perhaps it says, "Go to sleep, darlings, till the summer comes again."

—LEWIS CARROLL

We surrender and we accept. Then what happens? We experience a flow of grace. We align our will with the will of the universe and—even to the most jaded among us—curiosity is the result. "Just what is up here?" we wonder as unexpected—uncontrolled—events come to pass. Today's catastrophe proves to be tomorrow's opportunity. The dire event has a silver lining. Relinquishing control, we find ourselves led—led in unexpected directions. Once again, the universe seems to be benevolent. Our attempts at control are suddenly seen as being counterproductive. And so, educated by apparent adversity into wisdom, we can say the serenity prayer with conviction. We find we can be given "the serenity to accept the things we cannot change, the courage to change the things we can, and—above all—the wisdom to know the difference."

WRITE FOR GUIDANCE

Fill in the following:

    1. I wish I could control . . .

    2. Something I cannot change is . . .

    3. Something I need to accept is . . .

Now, ask your guidance what you need to know about the issue you cannot control. What wisdom do you receive? Does it bring you peace?

GUIDED, MOMENT TO MOMENT

And then, I have nature and art and poetry, and if that is not enough, what is enough?

—VINCENT VAN GOGH

I teach tomorrow afternoon and so tonight I am troubled by anxiety. The class is my second on my new prayer book and I have spent the week preparing: reading and rereading the chapters involved, writing not one outline but two, neither one "good enough." Anxiety is my usual companion when I am teaching. I call my friends for prayers and they thankfully comply.

"It's my joy," Scottie tells me, lighting incense on my behalf. Jennifer "white-lights" me, invoking a protective shield and joy. Jacob Nordby invokes the aid of angels, powerful beings engaged on my behalf. Nick Kapustinsky focuses goodwill on my behalf. Laura Leddy and my daughter, Domenica, say a potpourri of prayers. Julianna McCarthy visualizes me seated around her healing campfire. With all these prayers on my behalf, I am still anxious. I add to them my own prayers asking to have my fear removed. And yet, and still, anxiety lingers. It will remain until I begin teaching and then I will experience calm.

"It's stage fright," Julianna advises me.

"It *is* stage fright," Nick concurs. An actor, like Julianna, he experiences "terror." Once the play is underway, he's fine—as I am once I'm actually teaching.

I consider myself fortunate that my friends sympathize with my anxiety. They do not say, "But you've taught so many times before." Instead they recognize that each engagement is unique—the first time with *this* audience.

I find my anxiety tiresome. It troubles my sleep the night before teaching. I often dream terrible dreams, dreams in which I cannot teach, dreams in which the audience cannot hear me or I cannot hear them. I wake early on teaching days, needing to go over my outlines one last time.

"You're brave," Julianna tells me, and it does take courage to stand in front of a class—often a large class—teaching. I rely upon my guidance to cue me: *this next.* Sometimes the cues point me in unexpected directions. *Open your class with poetry and singing.* And so I open my class as directed, with poetry and singing.

Do Q and A, I am often prompted, setting aside the fear, "What if I don't know the answer?" Midway through the class, I find myself improvising, straying from my careful outline. I risk a novel direction. I ask the class to "fill in the blank," giving them a prompt that has suddenly come to me. By now, the class has taken off and all my anxiety seems foolish. I find myself feeling strong, in my element. I belatedly recognize that my teaching assignment was God's will for me. Maybe next time there will be no anxiety.

The evening is crystalline. The sun sets in ribbons of color. It is the end of a good day. I taught and the teaching went well. My class declared itself satisfied. I had carried a message of hope. "Prayers of petition" was my topic and I talked of our being able to count on a benevolent God. As we asked for our wants and our needs, we could have an expectation that God would fulfill our request with that or something better. In retrospect, God's will is always benign. And that is what I taught.

I firmly believe that nature can bring comfort to all who suffer.

—ANNE FRANK

Adopt the pace of nature: her secret is patience.

—RALPH WALDO EMERSON

Teaching, I could feel the alert attention of my class. I spoke of our need for a benevolent God, our need to move past an authoritarian God to a God of love. Just how do we move onward, I asked and answered. Begin by enumerating the negative traits you believed God to embody. Next number the positive traits you would desire your higher power to have. Listing the positives, we inch toward accepting them. We begin to conceive of the possibility that God is benevolent—kind, understanding, loving. This new God has our best interests at heart. Faced with a prayer of petition, this God considers carefully our well-being. We are given what we need, which may not be what we want, but is in fact something better.

It is thrilling to teach of a benevolent God. Deep inside the heart of every human is the desire for just such a God. Affirming that this is in fact the nature of God, I find myself happy. I am, after all, sharing good news and my students are happy to hear it. "Trust in a benevolent God," I tell them, and my words work alchemy. The harsh concepts they have harbored begin to be dissolved. Speaking the truth of God's nature is a powerful medicine, healing wounds that they have carried.

For it is wounding to believe in a negative God. Our very souls shrink at this concept. If we cannot believe in God's true nature, we find ourselves deeply, secretly pained. If we cannot believe that God is all loving, then we cannot find ourselves lovable. Believing that we are unlovable, we suffer. A negative God holds sway over ourselves and our destinies. Faced with such a God, we despair.

How much change is wrought as we rework our concept of God? A God that is friendly is great cause for optimism. Our will and God's will are no longer at opposite ends of the table. "May my will be thy will," we pray, and we experience a sense of rightness as we seek to align our will with a generous God. No longer adversarial, we experience a sense of kinship. Our hopes and desires are God-given, no longer a source of shame.

As we surrender our dreams to a benevolent God, we come to see surrender in a positive light. We accept our lot as God's beloved creatures. We hold fast to a belief in our essential goodness. Our dreams come from God and God has the power to accomplish them. Surrendering to God's timing, we experience an active faith. We see, in our surrender, hope. Each tomorrow holds the possibility of a better day. We surrender our sense of urgency and we receive peace. Accepting life as it unfolds turns out to be the firm bedrock of a happier existence. Trusting that God has our best interests at heart, we surrender to God's evident will. Our acceptance of things as they are allows the hand of God the freedom to act in our lives. And God, acting in our lives, brings us joy.

Nightfall is inky black. No moon is visible. The stars are candles in the night. My good day draws to a close. I love teaching and I love teaching what I am teaching: God is benevolent. We can rely on this great fact.

WRITE FOR GUIDANCE

Take pen in hand, and describe a situation that brings you anxiety or that you find tricky to navigate. Is it possible to ask for guidance in real time as you next encounter this situation? I often pause, listen, and am then clear about what to do next. The next time you encounter a complex situation, see if you can try asking for "moment to moment" guidance. How does it affect your experience, your clarity, and your actions? Do you feel yourself partnered by a benevolent energy?

A human being . . . experiences himself, his thoughts and feelings as something separate from the rest—a kind of optical delusion of his consciousness. The striving to free oneself from this delusion is the one issue of true religion.

—ALBERT EINSTEIN

THE POWER OF GRATITUDE

We know that God is everywhere; but certainly we feel His presence most when His works are on the grandest scale spread before us; and it is in the unclouded night-sky, where His worlds wheel their silent course, that we read clearest His infinitude, His omnipotence, His omnipresence.

—CHARLOTTE BRONTË

The sky is an azure blue bowl. The mountains stand out against it crisp and bold. The temperature is balmy, neither hot nor cold. Lily basks in the day's glow, stretching out on the deck, calm and peaceful. After the turbulent weather of the days past, today's beauty is restful, a cause for gratitude. "The weather," I write, listing my gratitudes. The weather is number one. Moving on, I write, "I'm grateful for my sobriety." It has been forty-two years since my last debauch. In that time, sobriety has been a constant, a firm foundation for my happy and useful life.

My gratitude list continues: "My health." At age seventy-two, I am blessed by robust health; save for the occasional backache, I am fit as a fiddle. All around me friends suffer maladies that I have escaped. As I write this Daniel is in the hospital with pneumonia, having survived an invasive surgery for cancer. His wife, Lucinda, hovers by his side. Her gratitude list enumerates, "Daniel's survival."

I pray daily for a couple of my acquaintance, Dusty and Arnold. Dusty suffers from Alzheimer's and Arnold suffers from lung cancer. I ask that they receive "all good things, all blessings, everything they need." My prayers are steady—steadier than their waning health.

And so when I list "my health" on my gratitude list, I recall the ailments I have to date eluded. What is a backache compared to cancer?

"My home," I write next, taking in my snug surroundings, cool in summer, warm in winter—lovely. My fireplace dominates the living room, making a welcome glow. My Audubon prints adorn the walls, mementos of my father's love for birds.

"Lily, my little dog" is next on the list although perhaps she should rank higher. Seven years old, in perfect health, she is a cheery companion. I think of my friend Todd's dog, Louie. Lily's age, he is beset by cancer. Todd sees him through, a day at a time, judiciously doling out pain meds. Yes, I am grateful for Lily's health.

But what is this? My gratitude list is a jumble. My daughter and granddaughter put in an appearance. Ditto for my beloved friend Emma Lively. After them, I have a list of friends, earning their place by their loyalty and longevity. Take my friend Gerard, an intimate for fifty-two years, calm, steady, insightful, irreplaceable for his good sense and even temper. Yes, I am grateful for my friends.

My gratitude list grows from ten to twenty to more. Listing each entry, another comes to mind. I list my hair, my skin, my limbs. My eyes, my nose, my mouth. And I have lovely hands for which I am grateful. Starting with a handful of gratitudes, I see the possibility of a hundred. And as I write my mood rises. My friend Jennifer advises me always, "Make a gratitude list. It combats depression." And so it does. I list my piñon tree, gently bobbing in the wind. I list ravens, hawks, coyotes—all the denizens of my domain.

As twilight falls, the earth cools—good sleeping weather for which I am grateful. The day winds down on a grace note.

To the eyes of the man of imagination, nature is imagination itself.

—WILLIAM BLAKE

Heaven is under our feet as well as over our heads.

—HENRY DAVID
THOREAU

Gratitude colors my perceptions. There is so much to be grateful for. My list expands to encompass my good life. As Jennifer counseled, gratitude fights depression. Depression becomes miniaturized and that note becomes cause for more gratitude. The moon rising over the mountains finds me with a grateful heart. Its beauty stirs the embers of my soul. My guidance tells me to write on gratitude. I have been obedient and a buoyant mood is the result. *Gratitude serves you,* my guidance advised me. I found this to be true.

TWILIGHT TURNS THE sky lilac. A deeper purple, the mountains loom high and majestic. The moon rises above their peaks. It is a tranquil evening. "Thank you, God," I pray, "for my good day." I received news of a book sale I was not expecting. My guidance proclaimed, *Much goodness flows to you,* and I wondered if the goodness was cash on the barrelhead. Perhaps so.

My day was bountiful not only in monetary terms. As I made my way through my day, I experienced an answered prayer. I fell asleep late last night, 2:00 A.M., and I asked for stamina to see me through my day. My prayer was answered by a rush of energy. I read and outlined a long chapter in the prayer book that I was teaching. The outline came together quickly and efficiently. I prayed to be guided and guided I was.

The chapter I worked on was "Prayers of Gratitude." Going over the chapter, point by point, I found my own gratitude increasing. To begin with, there was gratitude for the beauty found in nature. Ravens, hawks, tiny songbirds—each had a unique beauty. The soaring mountains, the swiftly passing clouds, how lovely! And next we have gratitude for homelier things—our health, our homes, our pets, our friends. Numbering our blessings, they multiply. A gratitude list that begins with ten is soon far too short as our gratitudes climb ever upward. I am grateful for my piñon tree, looming lush in every weather.

Finishing my outline, I said to Nick, "Let's walk Lily." And so we set out up the dirt road, climbing. The late afternoon was cool and Lily scampered ahead the length of her leash. Gone was the summer's heat which found her panting. Gone, too, were the summer's lizards which led her on a merry chase. Fall was in the air. I breathed a prayer of gratitude. "Thank you, God, for the cool." After the summer's heat, it came as a welcome relief.

Turning back toward home, Lily strained at her leash, as eager to be home as she had been to go out. Nick tugged on her leash—"Slow down"—and she reluctantly obeyed. We opened the courtyard gate and she abruptly braced her legs, not quite ready to go in lest there be one lingering lizard for her to chase. "This way, girl," Nick coaxed.

Back inside, I took stock of the day's events. My reading and my outline were work well done. My stamina was a welcome surprise. "Thank you, God," I breathed, settling in on my loveseat, appreciating the lilac sky. Dusk was lovely and the day had been good.

Walk as if you are kissing the Earth with your feet.

—THÍCH NHẤT HẠNH

A BRISK BREEZE stirred the piñon tree. The afternoon was cool and Lily hurried on her walk. No lizards were on view and Lily seemed to have forgotten them, brusquely rushing ahead, not pausing to hunt.

"Look! A rainbow!" Nick exclaimed and pointed to the mountains where a colorful arch appeared. "And look! There!" He pointed now to where a flock of birds had settled on a power line.

"Good spotting!" I told him. I enjoyed Nick's alert attention. It made of our daily dog walks an adventure.

"This way, Lily," I caroled to my briskly trotting dog. Did she

Cultivate the habit of being grateful for every good thing that comes to you; and . . . give thanks continuously.

And because all things have contributed to your advancement, you should include all things in your gratitude.

—WALLACE D. WATTLES

notice the rainbow? Lily skidded to a stop beneath the power line with its host of birds. "This way, girl," I egged her on. Reluctantly, she obeyed. The birds, after all, were far overhead. Not a likely snack. Back at home, dog treats awaited her, tiny, liver-flavored crackers, her favorites. Nick took a handful of treats and tossed them one at a time. Their game was interrupted by a ringing phone. The caller was Jennifer in sunny South Florida.

"How are you?" she asked breathlessly.

"I'm good," I told her. "Nick and I saw a rainbow today."

My phone rang again. "It's me, Ezra," announced artist Ezra Hubbard. "I'm in your courtyard. I have a ristra. I'll need a nail."

I opened the door to the courtyard and met up with a grinning Ezra cradling a three-foot string of red peppers, a "ristra."

"For you," he said. "Here, let me hang it." He located a nail in my portal and hung the colorful gift where it caught the afternoon light. Ristras are expensive and Ezra's gift was extravagant.

"And I brought you something else. It's a berry pie baked by the Mennonites in Colorado."

"Ezra, you're spoiling me," I protested, accepting the pie from his hands.

I ushered Ezra into the house and he promptly exclaimed over its newly painted interior. "I love it. With the colors, it's really your house."

We sat at the dining room table where we each eagerly devoured a slice of the pie.

"This is delicious!" I exclaimed, helping myself to a second slice. I felt the sugar jolting through my system. As a rule, I avoided sweets, but the Mennonite pie was irresistible.

"It's so good to have you here, Ezra," I told him. At forty-six years of age, Ezra was a lean and handsome man. We had known each other since he was sixteen, a lean and handsome youth. He lived in Florida now and his visit was unexpected.

"How goes the work?" I asked him.

"Oh, it's good. I have a mentor now, an older artist, and he keeps me on the straight and narrow."

"It's good you have an older man in your life."

"Yes," Ezra agreed. Raised by a single mother as a fatherless boy, Ezra hungered still for a father figure and now he had one.

A tiny alarm sounded from Ezra's wristwatch.

"Oops! Time to go!"

"Already?" I would have kept Ezra hours longer.

"I'm afraid so. Enjoy the rest of the pie."

"Oh, I will."

With that I ushered Ezra goodbye. It was twilight now and Lily was ready for an evening meal.

"Here, girl," I coaxed. "Dinner."

WRITE FOR GUIDANCE

As we name and enumerate our gratitudes, they do seem to multiply. Opening ourselves to seeing the good, more good flows to us. Take pen in hand and quickly fill in the following:

1. I'm grateful that . . .
2. I'm grateful that . . .
3. I'm grateful that . . .
4. I'm grateful that . . .
5. I'm grateful that . . .
6. I'm grateful that . . .
7. I'm grateful that . . .
8. I'm grateful that . . .
9. I'm grateful that . . .
10. I'm grateful that . . .
11. I'm grateful for . . .
12. I'm grateful for . . .
13. I'm grateful for . . .
14. I'm grateful for . . .

Acknowledging the good that is already in your life is the foundation for all abundance.

—ECKHART TOLLE

Let gratitude be the
    pillow
Upon which you kneel to
Say your nightly prayer
And let faith be the
    bridge
You build to overcome
    evil
And welcome good

    —MAYA ANGELOU

15. I'm grateful for . . .
16. I'm grateful for . . .
17. I'm grateful for . . .
18. I'm grateful for . . .
19. I'm grateful for . . .
20. I'm especially grateful for . . .

INVITING COMMITMENT

In this final week, you will come to value perseverance. You will deepen your practice of writing for guidance, and hopefully commit to it as a long-term habit. By now, guidance may seem second-nature, and you may have had enough experiences to convince you that it is not, in fact, your imagination—and that it is a valuable tool to use in every aspect of your life. Mentally, physically, and emotionally, guidance brings you valuable balance. The simple question "What next?" helps us to set our priorities in order. Guidance tutors us in the next right action. And so, what next? Ask your guidance.

PRAYER

The wind is gusting sixty miles per hour. The temperature has plunged forty degrees. Rain is predicted by nightfall and it is said to continue for two days. My power blinked out, shutting down my air conditioners, but I won't be needing them tonight. If anything my house will be too cool.

My friend Scottie phones me from San Diego, where it is eighty. She keeps an eye on Santa Fe weather. She wants to warn me of the impending cold snap and the stormy weather predicted. She keeps an eye out for my well-being. "I'll light some incense on your behalf," she tells me. "For your weather and for your writing." I thank her for her concern. It feels good to be looked after. Night is falling fast and a last glimpse at the darkening sky shows storm clouds.

Weather aside, the day felt turbulent. I reread my book on prayer, preparing for next Sunday's teaching. The chapters I read were on prayers of petition, asking God for what we want, presuming God's benevolence and generosity. Prayers of petition take daring. We stand naked before our maker asking for a boon.

Each one has to find his peace from within. And peace to be real must be unaffected by outside circumstances.

—MAHATMA GANDHI

God has three answers for us: yes, no, and not now. Praying, we hope for an affirmative. God's denial or delay demands our acceptance and understanding. The wisdom of God's answer is often revealed only later, in cozy retrospect.

Reading about prayers of petition, I felt myself vulnerable—as if I were praying, not merely reading. God almighty is the giver of all graces. Asking for a desire, we acknowledge that God is all powerful, able to grant—or not grant—our heartfelt wishes. And if God denies our request, we feel anger or, at best, frustration. We need to remind ourselves of God's wisdom and benevolence. God is all merciful, we need to affirm.

Reading over the chapter I had written, I reminded myself that my intention in writing about prayer was to render prayer easier, less daunting than is commonly felt. Prayers of petition are human and understandable, I wrote. We lay our requests at the feet of a compassionate God. That God knows the secrets of our hearts.

"Please keep me safe in the storm," I petition God now as night falls and the first drops of rain streak my windows. My friend Scott Thomas phones me to say the storm is hitting hard at his house—is it at mine? I tell him about my power blinking off, blessedly back on again in moments. "You're not in the dark, then?" he asks.

"No. I'm fine. And I have flashlights and candles," I reassure him.

"Just checking on you," he says, and I feel the glow of his concerned affection.

I live alone and the calls from my friends keep me from feeling isolated.

"Just checking on you," Emma Lively phones to say. She keeps a close tab on my well-being. "Did you drink enough water today?" she asks.

"I'll drink some now," I promise her, adding that water is

coming down in sheets, drenching the last embers of last week's fire.

"I've got you in prayers," she tells me next. I feel her goodwill.

The storm rattles the windows and shakes the chimney. I petition God, one more time, just to get his attention. "Please, God, keep me and my little dog safe." I feel the calm of an answered prayer.

THE FIRST WEEK of September I woke to discover snow had fallen during the night. My piñon tree was draped in white. My courtyard glistened with several inches of snow. Fog blotted out the mountains as on their slopes more snow was falling.

"Damn it!" I breathed, greeting the snowfall with dismay. Last year's winter was severe and long. I wasn't ready for another harsh season.

"I'm sad and dismayed," I wrote in my Morning Pages. I wanted sympathy for my bleak mood. Who could I call? I settled on Scottie in sunny San Diego, but she proved a bad choice. When I complained of the early snow, she sang, "Enjoy the beauty!" Hardly a sympathetic note.

Only one who attempts the absurd is capable of achieving the impossible.

—MIGUEL DE UNAMUNO

Next I tried Jennifer in sunny South Florida. She was more understanding. "It will pass," she advised me, and it did help to think of the snow as a passing anomaly, not the harbinger of more snow and cold.

"It's a cold snap," pronounced my neighbor Michele Warsa, emphasizing the fact that soon it would once again be warm. "Snap" implied rapidity. The snow would soon be gone. It was Michele's birthday and she did not complain of the weather. Was she a preternaturally good sport or did she welcome winter despite our abbreviated fall?

The day stayed gray. The fog thickened. At twilight there was a peal of thunder and rain fell in place of snow—wet, chill,

Remember, no effort that we make to attain something beautiful is ever lost.

—HELEN KELLER

unwelcome. As the temperatures dropped with nightfall, the rain jelled into snow. The world was once again turning white. "Enjoy the beauty," I scolded myself with Scottie's words. I called my friend Scott Bercu, a native New Yorker.

"It snowed!" I wailed. "It's snowing."

"So we heard," Scott replied. "An early winter?"

"I hope not. Last year was hard and I've been hoping this year would be mild."

"It's beyond our control," Scott spoke gravely.

"I've been fighting with God all day," I told him.

"Tomorrow might be better," Scott promised.

"Your voice to God's ear," I responded.

Nightfall was quick and inky black. The fog obscured the moon. A long peal of thunder announced the storm's continuing. The predictions were for continued rain mixed with snow. By week's end—and not before—the weather would relent.

ASKING FOR GUIDANCE, I am told to write about rest and relaxation and so I shall. Seeking guidance, I find it comes to me most easily when I am rested and relaxed. And so today I hear, *Talk about ease.*

As if sensing my relief, Lily stretches out languorously on the cool tile floor. I have found her ESP to be excellent. When I am anxious, she is anxious. When I am calm, as now, she is calm. Nightly I ask for guidance and when I am calm, it comes easily: *All is well.* I would venture that calm is a prerequisite of effective prayer.

"We have to stay positive," declares Scott Thomas, who calls nightly and practices what he preaches. "Negativity just breeds negativity and we have to avoid that." Scott's voice is calm and firm. He prays daily for guidance and his prayers to the ancestors are rewarded by a flow of direction for his days. "It was smoky today," he tells me. "The mountains looked hazy." His voice holds a rumble of concern. His nightly phone call reports a productive day. His guidance leads him to productivity. His calm lends itself to focus. All is well with him as he practices his daily Lakota rituals, praying to the ancestors and receiving their care. His guidance comes to him easily. The reward for his faithful prayer.

My phone shrills. The caller is Laura Leddy, another calm practitioner of daily prayer. "How are you?" she wants to know. "How is teaching going?"

"So far, so good," I tell her, pleased that she asks.

"I have you in prayers," she tells me and I know that Laura's prayers are powerful, steady, and calm.

"Thanks for the booster," I tell her, ever grateful for her prayers. Her voice is soft and gentle. Her manner is the same.

"I'm always glad to pray for you," Laura says firmly. I thank her once again and we end the call.

Nightfall cloaks the mountains. I am grateful to have heard from friends, grateful my friends are prayerful. Obeying my guidance, I am rested and relaxed. I hear: *Little one, you are on track. All is well.* Calm and centered, I say, "Thanks."

WRITE FOR GUIDANCE

Fill in the following:

1. I would like to petition God to . . .

2. I am fighting with God over . . .

3. I felt a sense of ease when . . .

Now, write for guidance on these issues. What do you hear? Do you get a sense that God's timing may indeed be the best timing? Can a connection to your guidance bring you ease and grace?

Follow your bliss and don't be afraid, and doors will open where you didn't know they were going to be.

—JOSEPH CAMPBELL

THE EASE OF A SUPPORTIVE NETWORK

"I'm just checking on you," Jennifer tells me. "Are you well?"

"I'm fine," I answer, hoping my voice has the lilt of optimism.

"Well then, I'll talk to you tomorrow," Jennifer promises, ringing off.

The call—and the checkup—are welcome. Separated as we are by thousands of miles—Jennifer is in Florida; I am in New Mexico—our telephone contact is critical to our sense of well-being. Recently Jennifer suffered a severe allergic reaction to a new medication. She broke out in terrible welts that burned and itched. Hearing her long-distance report, I worried. And so I called her twice daily, just to check on her.

With my friendships far-flung—Andrew in London, Emma in New York, Laura in Chicago—I make a point of telephone calls and cards, all saying, "I love you. I miss you. How are you?" I try to call, if not daily, often. My guidance tells me, *Be loving. Be verbal.* And so I am.

"How are you?" my beloved mentor Julianna asks me when I have called to check on her.

"I'm good," I say, feeling better for having made our connection. Julianna has been a constant presence in my life for forty-one years. Now that we have Zoom, I see her, not just hear her. At ninety-one she is, in her words, "a crone," but her beloved face belies the years. I'm so grateful for our contact.

Your beloveds are safe in my keeping, guidance assures me, but I pray near daily for their health and well-being. I am relieved, talking to Gerard, to hear him "steady as he goes." A temperate man, he fields my weekly calls with good humor. *He fares well,* my guidance tells me and Gerard himself says the same.

Most of my friendships are decades long but my new friend, writer Jacob Nordby, has earned a place in my heart. Jacob is a calm and loving presence, assuring me of my place in his prayers. He prays for me when I'm teaching or when I have a difficult interview. I am grateful for his spiritual intercession on my behalf. My guidance tells me he is a *kindred spirit,* and so I find him.

Trust your network, guidance advises me, and so I do. Writing of friendship, I think of Jeannette who repeatedly assures me, "You are not alone." And I'm not. Accompanied by my far-flung friends, I live alone but not in isolation. Our love and loyalty connect us and so when Jennifer calls "just to check on me," I truthfully say, "I'm fine."

If the only prayer you said in your whole life was, "Thank You," that would suffice.

—J. JOHN AND
MARK STIBBE

SMOKE FROM CALIFORNIA fires has drifted all the way to New Mexico. Walking Lily, my eyes sting, although Nick says his eyes aren't bothered. Blinking against the smoky wind, I ask Nick how he is doing. "Fine," he declares, his voice firm and steady. We walk Lily for half an hour and if the smoke is bothering her, she doesn't show it. Back at home, I am grateful to be back in air-conditioned splendor, away from the smoke. My eyes burn and I look out the windows to the west where a fiery sun is setting. The sky burns reddish-orange. Smoke is the cause.

Entering the house, my phone shrills. The caller is Scott Thomas, reporting in on a long—and smoky—day. "Did you see the sunset?" he asks. "The smoke turns the sky orange."

"I saw it," I say. "And I felt it. Walking Lily, my eyes stung."

"Mine were okay," Scott reports. "There must be more smoke up where you are."

"Yes. I think so," I say.

"So it's fall. The pear tree's leaves are red and gold."

"I'm dreading winter," I confess.

"Oh, dear. You have to accept it—the calm and the beauty."

"The cold," I complain.

"Yes, well, there's that." Scott chuckles. He is resigned to the coming cold. Agreed to disagree on the approaching season, we get off the phone. As soon as I put the receiver back in its cradle, the phone shrills again. This time the caller is Jennifer, checking in on me again.

"I'm fine," I tell her. "But my eyes sting. There's smoke in the air."

"Not another fire," Jennifer exclaims.

"Smoke from California's fires," I exclaim.

"That's a pity. How's Lily?"

"She seems fine. The smoke didn't seem to bother her."

"That's just great. Can you rinse your eyes?"

"I could."

"I think it would help."

As always, Jennifer is filled with advice. I am four days into using the MA roller she prescribed for my back.

"It will change your life," she told me, and using it—a painful process—my back pain afterward is lessened. And so, welcoming Jennifer's pragmatism, I rinse my eyes. As she predicted, it helps.

"Better?" she asks.

"Better," I tell her. We get off the phone both feeling better for her advice.

Lily licks her paws. Maybe there is a smoky tang clinging to her coat. She climbs next to me on the arm of the loveseat. Her breathing is deep and even. She is relaxed.

"Treat, Lily?" I ask her and together we pad to the kitchen. I scoop up a handful of her liver-flavored treats. One at a time I send them skittering across the floor and Lily scampers after them.

"A good day, eh, girl, despite the smoke?" I close the dog door, shutting her in for the night.

WRITE FOR GUIDANCE

List three supportive people in your network.

Now, list three people you could offer support to.

Ask your guidance:

1. Who should I reach out to for support?

2. Who should I reach out to in order to offer my support?

Reach out to these people and note what happens. Do you experience synchronicity or sense a higher hand at play?

The truth about life and lie about life is not measured by others but by your intuition, which never lies.

—SANTOSH KALWAR

HOLDING THE FAITH

In a time of destruction,
create something.

—MAXINE HONG
KINGSTON

I taught today and taught well. My guidance was clear and sharp: *Open the class with poetry and song.* I did as directed, reading two poems from my collection *This Earth,* then singing a song of wisdom, "Time Is Like a River." Although I could not see my class, I could sense them and we launched from there into the deep end with questions on prayers of gratitude: starting with the beauties of the natural world, we listed our blessings. I could feel the intense focus of the group. Blessings listed raised the energy of the students. The afternoon sped past.

Now it is evening and as dusk settles it brings with it calm. Tiny birds flit to the piñon tree. They will rest in its branches overnight. Lily has also found a resting spot, curling up on the living room's colorful rug. With all the world easing into nightfall, I seek guidance on the day's events.

Julia, your class went well. There is no cause for anxiety. You were smooth and helpful.

Perhaps so, but I feel no elation over a job well done.

Instead, I feel empty—hollow, devoid of emotion. Perhaps I am tired. Perhaps the class took all of my energy. I lie down to rest but the phone shrills. Groggy, I answer it. The caller is my daughter, wanting to know how the day's teaching went.

"It went well," I tell her. "Both Emma and Nick said so, but I feel empty."

"Do you want feedback?"

"Okay."

"I think it's a performance thing. When I do a play, there are nights when I feel empty afterward and it has nothing to do with the quality of my work. People assure me my performance was fine. I am just numb. My energy is spent. It happens."

I'm grateful for my daughter's diagnosis. It makes my mood a normal thing. If my nerves before teaching are stage fright, my lack of emotion afterward is a letdown performers also experience. I don't have a name for it but it's part of a performer's life cycle. While I hadn't thought of teaching as a performance, clearly it was.

One more time, my guidance has something to say. *You are needing help to have an overview. For today try to believe Nick and Emma. They felt you did well and they are both honest. You are tired and wired. You taught well and now you can release your anxiety.*

When the guidance names my mood "anxiety," I realize that I am not so much empty as anxious. I want to be reassured that my class was indeed good and not flat as my emotions would have me fear. Perhaps it is normal to want reassurance, but I find my insecurity tiresome. Shouldn't I be able to keep my own counsel? One more time, I turn to guidance. I hear: *Julia, you are a perfectionist and you want assurance your class was perfect. Allow yourself to be human. Lower the bar. Accept that your class was good—good enough. And good enough is more than good enough.*

Good advice and wise counsel. Now, if I can just take it! As

Only thoughts that come by walking have any value.

—FRIEDRICH NIETZSCHE

I only went out for a walk, and finally concluded to stay out till sundown, for going out, I found, was really going in.

—JOHN MUIR

if to console me, Lily pads to my side. All is well, her presence assures me. And, indeed, all is well.

ONE MORE DAY of smoky wind. Walking Lily, my eyes sting again. This time, I cut our walk short. The smoke is too much for me.

Safely back inside the house, I phone Jennifer, knowing she will have compassion for my stinging eyes.

"Smoky again?" she asks.

"Yes," I tell her dolefully.

"As bad as yesterday?"

"Bad enough," I answer. "I think I need patience. Surely the smoke will clear soon."

"Your voice to God's ear," Jennifer says gravely. "Meanwhile, rinse your eyes and keep an eye on Lily."

Getting off the phone, I do keep an eye on Lily. She seems unfazed although perhaps annoyed by our abbreviated walk. She stretches out beside me on the loveseat, a comforting presence. "Good girl," I tell her.

Jacob Nordby calls me next from Boise, Idaho. He reports that Boise is now smoke-free, having been bedeviled as badly as Santa Fe by smoke drifting in from the west. "I'm going for a hike," Jacob reports. "The air quality is good again."

"We're still smoky," I tell him, self-pity saturating my tone.

"I hope it clears for you soon," Jacob sympathizes. "I hate to hear you suffering." Compassion rumbles through the wire. Jacob is a kind man and an empathetic one. I'm grateful for his concern. Envying him his clear skies, I wish him happy hiking. There is no hiking for me here in smoky Santa Fe.

Taking pen to page, I next query guidance: "What to do about the smoke?" I am told: *Julia, the smoke will clear. Try to have patience. There is nothing to be gained by agitation. Stay indoors and avoid the smoky wind. Soon enough the skies will one more time be clear.*

And so, tutored to have patience, I look to the mountains and discover them hazy but sharply etched. The smoke is lessening. Soon, like Jacob, I will be able to go hiking. Santa Fe, like Boise, will have clear skies.

One more time, the tiny birds flit into the piñon tree's inner recesses. A lone raven circles the tree but doesn't land. Evening is settling. I get one more call, this one from Corey, a girlfriend. She reports sadly that she has encountered a flock of dead sparrows on her property. Victims of smoky air? I wonder. Delicate creatures to be sure. I recall passing the tiny corpse of a songbird as I walked Lily. Its chest was red and gold, the colors of the setting sun, as if the bird were a tiny particle of the sunset fallen to earth. Now a half-moon rises above the mountains. I call Lily indoors and lock her dog door. It's time for bed. Perhaps tomorrow will be better.

Walking . . . is how the body measures itself against the earth.

—REBECCA SOLNIT

THE SUN IS setting in colored ribbons. The moon is rising in the east. I put pen to page inquiring, "What shall I write about?" The answer comes back to me: *Faith.* It takes faith to write about faith, to believe that my pen will be led. I have years of experience working with guidance but still I hesitate, my pen hovering above the page. What is there to say about faith? A great deal.

Another word for faith is "trust," and trust is something built over time. My guidance says, *You are well and carefully led.* And so I put pen to page asking, "In what direction?" A word at a time, a thought at a time, the answer is revealed. I am asked to have faith in my own unfolding wisdom. I am told that faith equals trust equals security in an unknown future.

All is well, my guidance tells me, and so I strive to believe in benevolence. For forty-two years I have followed a spiritual path and despite my fears and doubts, all *has* always been well. Perhaps it is because I have made a commitment. I have consciously turned "my will and my life" over to "the care of God." Ups and downs notwithstanding, I have always remembered my bargain. In dark times, I have asked, "I wonder what God is up to." In short, I practiced faith. My curiosity sought a silver lining and, sure enough, there was always one to be found.

As my experience built, faith became easier. God hadn't brought me this far to be dropped. *You are not abandoned,* my guidance promised me. The reassuring words gave me hope and hope in turn led to further faith.

My friend Jeannette tells me, "Guidance is always present." Depending on guidance, my faith is tested—and increased. I put pen to page asking to be led and guidance assures me, *You are led carefully and well.* Again the words invite faith forward. If I am indeed led "carefully and well," what is there to fear?

My friend the late Jane Cecil counseled me, "There's always a choice between faith and fear. Choose faith." And so I came to exercise a spiritual muscle. It took effort to choose faith but the effort was rewarding. Faith became a habit, a tested response to life. Faith built upon faith. Life was no longer a free fall. Faith was my parachute.

And so when I am directed to write about faith, I find myself brimming with optimism. The good news is that faith is available to all of us. At first a flyer into the unknown, it becomes with practice a chosen response to life. It allows us to meet apparent adversity with equanimity. If "faith without works is dead," it allows us to do works and hence become alive. Faith builds upon itself, creating more faith. We come to trust faith and rely upon it. And so the directive to write about faith becomes a task gladly undertaken. Faith, after all, is the good news. Believing in faith, I am indeed well and carefully led.

WRITE FOR GUIDANCE

Recall a time when you acted in faith. What was the result?

Now, bring pen to page, and fill in the following:

1. I had faith when . . .

2. I could use more faith around . . .

3. My guidance encourages me to have faith about . . .

THE POWER OF WALKING

Solvitur ambulando: *It is solved by walking.*

— ST. AUGUSTINE

It's midafternoon on a bright and sunny day when I set out with Lily for her daily walk. Opening the door to the courtyard, she scampers ahead of me, tugging at her leash. "Wait up, girl," I tell her, hurrying to match her strides. She understands my tone, if not my words, and slows her pace. I catch up to her and give her leash a tug to the right, heading up our dirt road, toward the juniper grove with its chorus of songbirds. They carol to us as we approach. Drawing abreast, they grow more muted. Passing the sibilant grove, we draw near a meadow, the site of many deer spottings, but today no deer are in sight. A single squirrel scurries ahead of us, dashing into the safety of one golden chamisa bush. A large rabbit is the next creature to appear. Lily yanks at her leash but the rabbit is too quick for her and so she drops back to my side, walking now at a dignified pace, depressed by her lack of luck hunting.

Distracted as I have been by Lily's antics, I find myself annoyed that my walk isn't its usual meditation. I am accustomed to walks bringing me guidance, and today I need the answers that walking can provide. I headed out with a question: "What shall I write about?" The question eddied in my consciousness as Lily tugged for my attention. As she settled down, matching her pace to my own, the question came into clear focus and, blessedly, with it came an answer, *Write about walking.*

Walking, I stretch my legs and my mind. Focused on my surroundings, I am cast into "the now." And it is there, in the precise present, that answers come to me. They come as the hunch, the inspiration, the inkling. The "still, small voice" grows amplified. A footfall at a time, trudging an earthly path, I walk my way into higher realms. I get a sense of a larger, benevolent something overarching my reality. This higher power gifts me with a sense of optimism and well-being. I am talked to—as writer Brenda Ueland, herself a great walker, put it—"by God and his messengers." Walking, I am receptive to higher forces. Walking, I switch my inner dial over from "send" to "receive." And what I receive is a wisdom greater than my own.

Heading back toward home, Lily strains at her leash. As eager as she was to go out, she is now eager to go home. Once more she hastens her pace and once more I rein her in. I walk slowly and deliberately. My direction, *Write about walking,* has filled me with thoughts. I turn them over as we open the garden gate. Crossing the courtyard, I have a sense of satisfaction. Lily dawdles by my rose bushes. "Come on, girl," I urge her, opening the door. Our walk has been a good one after all.

I shall wear white flannel trousers, and walk upon the beach.

—T. S. ELIOT

THE LITTLE DOG is stretched out on the hardwood floor. She enjoys the cool of the air conditioning. It penetrates her thick coat and renders her comfortable despite the late summer's heat.

Now shall I walk
Or shall I ride?
"Ride," Pleasure said;
"Walk," Joy replied.

—W. H. DAVIES

"Here, girl," I coax her, patting a spot beside me on the love-seat. She hears me but she ignores me. She is comfortable as she is. She's had her dinner and a nap is called for. Later in the evening, she will be more compassionate. Right now, she is missing an air show. Ravens cruise past my windows. They light on the piñon tree, glistening ebony. I admire their hijinks as they bob with the wind.

Moving to Santa Fe ten years ago, I planned to live in town, walking distance to shops and cafes. That plan was scuttled when I rented my first house, three miles out of town, in a grove of juniper and piñon where wildlife flourished. I discovered I craved wilderness, not civilization. And two years ago I moved still farther from the downtown plaza to the house I eventually bought, a snug adobe featuring a courtyard and mountain views. This new house is surrounded by flora and fauna, flocks of ravens, strolling trios of deer. My living room window encompasses a grand vista. At night I enjoy moonrise over the mountains.

My courtyard is surrounded by a high adobe fence—no deterrent to squirrels and raccoons. The courtyard garden features iris, lily, and roses. Its stony floor has proved to be a basking place for lizards. A lone juniper tree stands sentinel near the house. Three birch trees make up a miniature grove in the far corner.

My house is shaped as a horseshoe circling the courtyard. From the portal I have hung the festive ristra, the gift from artist Ezra Hubbard. I have painted the interior vivid colors—lilac, aqua, and persimmon.

"Oh, I love the colors! Your house is lovely!" exclaimed painter Annie Brody, a recent visitor. She gifted me with a large purple orchid, "to keep you company while I'm out of town." The blooming plant complemented the lilac walls, hung with Audubon prints, an homage to my father's love of birds.

The piñon tree adjacent to my living room offers shelter to a bevy of tiny birds. They inhabit its innermost reaches, leaving the outer boughs to the ravens who peck like sentries on the lookout. Western tanagers and flickers often share their roosts. Seated on my loveseat, looking out, I am treated daily to an aviary show.

The back of my house is fenced for little Lily. The fence is high—six feet—an effective deterrent for coyotes and bears, a safe haven for Lily. Sometimes at night, coyotes prowl the fence line causing Lily to give a worried woof in response to their ghostly howls. In bear season, neighbors warn each other, "Beware," and so I practice alert caution pulling into my garage. Bears have been known to lurk by high adobe walls, seeking out forage. Caution is the watch word.

A three-quarters moon rises over the mountains tonight, its bright silver light shining in my windows. Dimmed by its light, the evening star is a mere candle. Lily, roused from her nap, pads to my bedroom where she takes comfort on a velvet coverlet. The evening is quiet. No coyotes visit. Moonlight bathes the courtyard and all is calm. At nine I will place a phone call to my friend Jeannette in New York. I picture her apartment, cozy amid glittering high-rises. She pictures my life here in Santa Fe. Our friendship spans the miles as Jeannette asks me, "Ready for bed?" Clad in pajamas and a fluffy bathrobe, I answer, "Yes," shutting the house down for the night, flicking off lights, shutting Lily's dog door. All is still as I bid Jeannette good night, grateful for the company our phone call has provided—grateful, too, for my solitary life in sylvan splendor.

Walking through darkness with thoughts full of colors.

—PRAJAKTA MHADNAK

WRITE FOR GUIDANCE

Take pen to page and write out a question that has been lingering. Listen to what you hear in response. Now, lace up your shoes and

*I have walked myself
into my best thoughts,
and I know of no
thought so burdensome
that one cannot walk
away from it.*

—SØREN KIERKEGAARD

go out for a solo walk—twenty minutes is enough. Bring your question with you on your walk.

When you return home, return once more to the page. What occurred to you as you walked?

THE BENEVOLENCE OF GUIDANCE

Lakota elder Scott Thomas calls for an abbreviated moment. "I know you need to write," he says. "I wish you guidance. I'll talk to you tomorrow." With that brief note of well wishing, he hangs up. I'm grateful for his call, comfortable in its intention. Scott intends me well and his wish for me to have guidance is welcome. Scott himself relies upon guidance coming to him daily from what he calls "the invisible world." Like me, he makes a practice of seeking counsel from those who have passed on and so his call to me tonight cues me to reach out to my deceased beloveds.

Write about benevolence, I hear first from my late friend Jane Cecil, who had an unshakable faith in the goodness of God. Living her life one day at a time, she always found the good in the day's unfolding. Call her with an apparent catastrophe and she'd point you to the silver lining. Worried about finances? "God will provide." Worried about health? "God is the dear and glorious physician." Worried, as I am now, about creativity, Jane

Prayer is not asking. Prayer is putting oneself in the hands of God, at His disposition, and listening to His voice in the depth of our hearts.

—MOTHER TERESA

To ease another's
heartache is to forget
one's own.

—ABRAHAM LINCOLN

assures me that the creator is a fountain of ideas, "Only tap in." God is benevolent, Jane believed—and believes still from her perch in the afterlife. When I ask her for guidance, I am told, *Julia, I am at your side.* And I do feel Jane is with me, a comforting presence ever assuring me of God's benevolence. I keep her picture on my refrigerator.

I next turn to the late Elberta Honstein, a breeder of championship Morgan horses. Like Jane, Elberta remains a vivid and spirited soul. Her language retains the flavor of the horse-show ring. *Julia, you are a champion,* she tells me. *I give you stamina and grace.* I confess to Elberta that I am nervous speaking and teaching, fatigued from a restless night's sleep caused by my anxiety. Elberta assures me, *You will do well.* In death as in life, Elberta is a staunch optimist. Her optimism brims over. *You are well led,* she states confidently. And her confidence, like Jane's faith, is catching. *All will be well,* I am told. I thank Elberta for her ease.

Benevolence and optimism characterize the messages I receive. My guidance is filled with hope—hope for a benevolent and optimistic future. I am tutored daily in positivity. Those who have passed on share their overview. Those who remain with me here in the visible world seek out higher realms and higher forces. Scott Thomas prays "to the ancestors, to the spirits." I pray to Jane and Elberta, to "higher forces," and, when I am bold enough, to the "higher power." No matter what name we choose, guidance is always available. As we avail ourselves of higher wisdom, we are led "carefully and well." We are assured, *Do not doubt our goodness. We intend you great good.* That and *there is no error in your path. Great goodness flows to you.* And so as we check in with higher forces we are assured of our future in higher realms. God indeed is benevolent and we have great cause for optimism.

*   *   *

NIGHT HAS FALLEN. A full moon rises over the mountains, luminous and pale. My phone shrills and the caller, one more time, is Scott Thomas, ever peaceful and calm. He is "just checking" on me, wondering if my day has gone well, which, blessedly, it has. I have walked on the treadmill, walked Lily, and worked out. My physical exertions give me endorphins, nature's booster rockets promoting well-being. I find myself optimistic and well balanced. All systems are "go" as I head into my evening's writing.

But what to write about? A single word of guidance comes to me: *candor.* Our world needs candor and candor can be cultivated. To be candid is to be authentic, to speak our truth without censorship. For many of us this is an elusive act. We filter our words through a screen of what we consider acceptable. Candor eschews such censorship. It demands that we consider all our promptings acceptable. Yes, even the ugly-duckling thoughts that we are tempted to hide.

How can we resist the temptation to tailor our thoughts? To begin with, we must practice self-acceptance, saying to ourselves, "All parts of me are welcome here." Such self-acceptance takes practice and we can best practice it through our Morning Pages.

Put simply, Morning Pages are an exercise in self-disclosure. Undertaken first thing upon awakening, before our defenses are in place, they tutor us in honesty and self-revelation. In the pages we are authentic and vulnerable. We write, "This is what I want more of. This is what I want less of." Our opinions and disclosures often surprise us. "I didn't know I felt that way!" we mentally exclaim. Nothing is off-limits. All thoughts are equally valid—joyous or disgruntled, happy or sad. There is no "wrong" way to write pages. They may be lively or loving, interesting or

Kind people are the best kind of people.

—AMIT KALANTRI

No one has ever become poor from giving!

—ANNE FRANK

dull. They give us a glimpse of our undefended mind. In a word, we are candid and the candor carries over from our writing into our speech. We find ourselves saying the previously unsayable. Honesty becomes our currency, authenticity the coin of the realm.

We experience a new freedom—and a new self-respect. As we speak our truth, we validate ourself and our perceptions. Others sense our solid core. We are trustworthy. Our candor yields us so. Writing our morning thoughts, we have become intimate with ourselves. Our self-intimacy renders us able to forge intimate bonds with others. As we become human to ourselves, we dare to be known to others. Our candor paves the way for authentic relationships. Like the full moon in the nighttime sky, we are clearly visible, shedding our light on those who surround us, gifting them with honesty and authenticity. "To thine own self be true," we pay attention to the dictum. True to ourselves, we are rendered true to others. Candor wins the day.

ASKING FOR AID for the many needs of my beloveds, I am assured, *Julia, your beloveds are in my custody and care.* I take up this cue, praying, "Dear God, please give everyone everything they need." I try not to dictate the details of my request. Tutored to pray for knowledge of God's will and the power to carry it out, I strive to align my will with the higher power. I do this by writing out my concerns and the guidance I receive. I am told, *Do not doubt my goodness,* and I realize that my faith in a benevolent God is something that I must daily reinforce by seeking still more guidance.

So now I ask: "Is there more for me to say about guidance?"

I hear, *Julia, you lead by example.*

And what is that example?

I practice asking for guidance at all turns, in all arenas of my life. There is nothing too small—or too large—to seek advice on. Take now: my guidance tells me my book is at an end. *Julia, I hear, you have demonstrated how guidance works in your life. Your readers can follow your lead.* At its core, writing for guidance acts on a desire for divine assistance, a reaching out beyond our human wisdom to a higher octave. All in all, this book seeks to demonstrate that guidance is available to each of us, on every topic, always.

WRITE FOR GUIDANCE

Look back through the guidance you have written. Does it have a tone of benevolence? Have you come to see, as I have, the value of asking for guidance in any and all aspects of our lives? It is my hope that you have shared in this comforting and helpful practice I use every day.

Moving forward, can you commit to daily Morning Pages and daily writing for guidance?

ACKNOWLEDGMENTS

Jennifer Bassey

Tyler Beattie

Scott Bercu

Sonia Choquette

Nick Kapustinsky

Rena Keane

Chris Kukulski

John Kukulski

Joel Fotinos

Laura Leddy

Emma Lively

Jacob Nordby

Scottie Pierce

Susan Raihofer

INDEX

ABOUT THE AUTHOR

Robert Stivers

Hailed by *The New York Times* as "The Queen of Change," **JULIA CAMERON** is credited with starting a movement in 1992 that has brought creativity into the mainstream conversation—in the arts, in business, and in everyday life. She is the bestselling author of more than forty-five books, fiction and nonfiction; a poet, songwriter, filmmaker, and playwright. Commonly referred to as "The God-mother" or "High Priestess" of creativity, she considers herself "the floor sample of her own toolkit" and her tools are based in practice, not theory. *The Artist's Way* has been translated into more than forty languages and sold more than five million copies to date.

Read more from
"The Queen of Change" (*New York Times*)
JULIA CAMERON!